DICE&LEAD

Issue 1
June 2024

Editor
Lorenzo Sartori

Assistant editors
Renato Genovese, Howard Meissel

Contributors (this issue)
Antonio Dimichele, Stefano Izzo, Marco Ortalda

3D Maps
Erregrafica

Advertising
Lorenzo Sartori
lorenzosartori67@gmail.com

Contributions in the form of articles, letters, reviews and news are welcomed. Please send to lorenzosartori67@gmail.com

Published by Lorenzo Sartori
Dad&Piombo Publishing

Printed by Amazon
ISBN: 9798327097308

Digial edition available through
Wargame Vault
https://www.wargamevault.com/

Copyright Lorenzo Sartori
All rights reserved. Nothing in this publication may be reproduced in any form without prior written consent of the publishers. Any individual providing material for publication must ensure that the corret permissions have been obtained before submission to us. Every effort has been made to trace copyrights holders, but in some cases this proves impossible. The editor/publisher apologize for any unwitting cases of copyright trangressions and would like to hear from any copyright holders not acknowledged. Articles and the opinions expressed herein do not necessarily represent the views of the editor/publisher.

BRIEF

What you see here is the first issue of the international edition of Dice&Lead. It is the child of Dadi&Piombo, Italy's first wargame magazine that is celebrating its 25th anniversary this year. The magazine has for sometime been published Italian but, for a brief period spanning issues 22 to 46, it was published in an Italian/English format. If you are interested, you can purchase those issues in pdf on Wargame Vault or write to us for hard copies. The dual language period was a very interesting time that allowed us to reach readers all over the world but we had to end it due to the prohibitive rise in shipping costs. The idea of returning to publishing the magazine in English, however, has always remained in our minds and the time is now ripe. In Dice&Lead you will find the best of the articles published previously only in Italian but also new material, so we are very open to receiving suggestions and collaborations from you.

Many of you might know Dadi&Piombo for its rulebooks, such as Impetus, Basic Impetus, Baroque, and Lords&Servants. One of the various goals of D&L is also to provide support for our games but not to the exclusion of any of the others.

D&L is not periodical, we plan to release a couple of issues a year, sometimes it may be only one and maybe the year after three. Distribution at the moment is through Amazon for the print version and Wargame Vault for the digital edition.

In this first briefing I think I have told you everything, so it only remains for me to wish you good reading.

Lorenzo Sartori
Spring 2024

Cover pic:
American militia at the battle of Cowpens.
Perry Miniatures from the collection of John Maguire.
Photo Nathan Vinson.

IN THIS ISSUE

4 The battle of Cowpens

34 Painting with contrast

17 The Late Roman army

40 The Hussites

23 Nördlingen 1634

51 Showcase

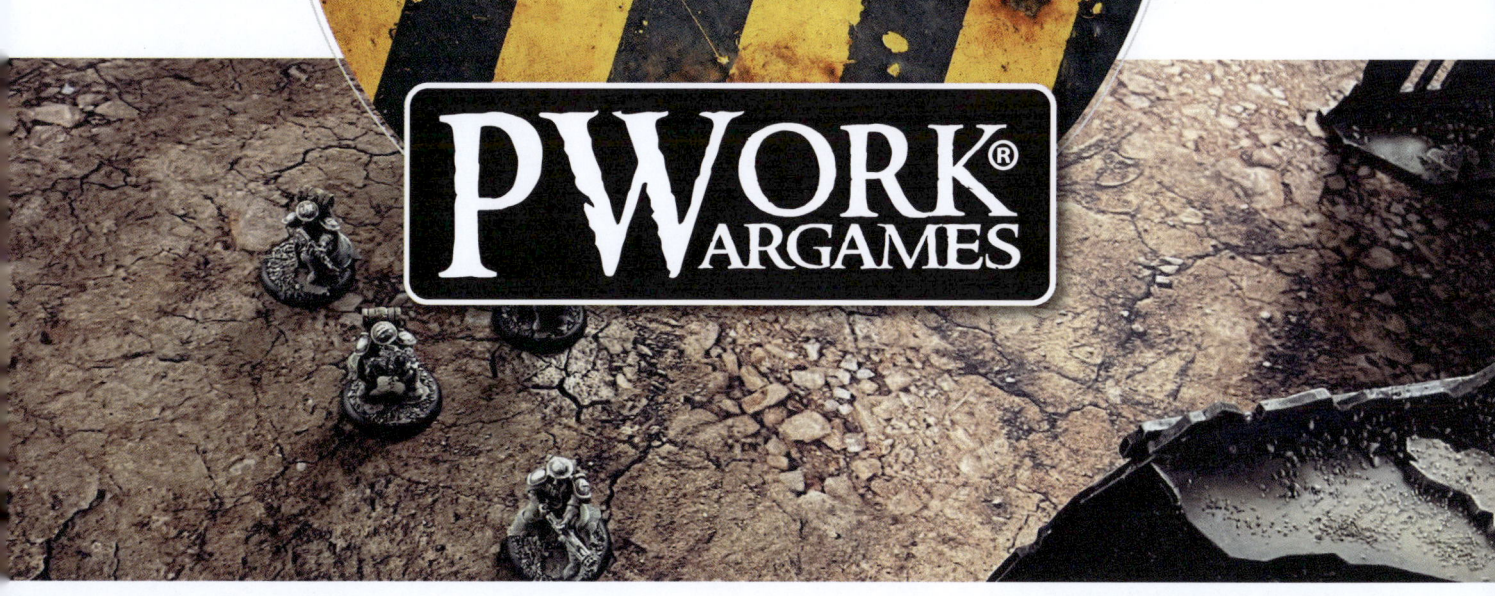

The battle of Cowpens

by HOWARD MEISSEL

The battle of Cowpens fought in South Carolina in 1781 has been described by some historians as a miniature Cannae where an American army executed a double envelopment that destroyed a British force. Fought in a remote frontier clearing it was, by European standards, a small battle involving only about three thousand combatants. Although this was a small battle involving small armies they were led by big personalities; Daniel Morgan and Banastre Tarleton were two of the most colorful leaders in the American War for Independence. The battle of Cowpens also had a significant impact on the war's final outcome.

THE STRATEGIC SITUATION

By 1779 Britain's war to regain control over its rebellious colonies had reached its fifth year. It had been five years of frustration for King George III and his government. British efforts to isolate New England from the other colonies had failed at Saratoga in 1777. This American victory had resulted in the surrender of a sizable British army and brought France into the war. The French promised to provide the Americans with supplies, troops, and ships to challenge the royal Navy's control of the 13 rebellious colonies' coast. In the meantime, a revised British strategy involving the capturing and occupation of colonial towns and cities in the central colonies had also failed to bring the American rebels to heel. Since then,

28mm Perry Miniatures. Collection John Maguire. Photo Nathan Vinson.

the main armies of both sides had settled down to a sort of stalemate, with George Washington's Continental Army encamped around the primary British base of operations in New York City. From his headquarters there, Henry Clinton, the commander in Chief of the British forces in America, recognized that a war of attrition favored the American or, "patriot" cause as it would eventually allow France to deploy its fleet and reinforce the rebels. His request to be relieved and return to England had been denied. Something needed to be done before the French army arrived in force and the Royal Navy's control of the seas was challenged. Clearly a new strategy to break the deadlock was needed.

THE PROMISE OF A SOUTHERN STRATEGY

Clinton turned his attention to the four southern colonies lying south of the Potomac river. South Carolina, North Carolina and Virginia had been the scene of British defeats in 1775 and 1776. In spite of this, 1778 had brought some successes there. In the sparsely settled colony of Georgia the principle city and port of Savannah was captured. This city provided a base of operations for moving up the Southern coast and into the interior. Clinton's emerging southern strategy was further supported by his belief that the south contained a significant number of discontented slaves and "Tories," a term for colonists loyal to the crown. Moreover, a major campaign there offered the possibility of shifting the American and French attention away from the New York standoff. There were also drawbacks to a southern strategy. Supplying a British army there would be difficult, the summers were blisteringly hot and unhealthy, towns and cities away from the coast were few and widely spread connected by a poor network of very rough roads that wandered through vast expanses of partisan infested swamps and forests. Any force operating there would be highly dependent on local Tories to provide aid as guides and auxiliary troops. It was a risk but Clinton was running out of options, in England the public was running out of patience and the government out of money.

A joint campaign conducted by the Americans and French to retake Savannah ended in disaster in October of 1779. Moreover, the failure to retake the city exposed serious problems in the Franco-American relationship involving coordination of forces and conflicting agendas. The positive results of the campaign for the British confirmed Clinton's belief about the vulnerability of the south as the successful defense of the city had been aided by sizable numbers of Loyalists and slaves. The French fleet departed the coast leaving behind a weakened American army that had no choice but to abandon most of the Georgia colony. For the patriots, the failure to retake Savannah was an early indication that American General Benjamin Lincoln commander in the south would not be clever or experienced enough to contend with the capable but cautious General Clinton or his experienced second in command Lord Charles Cornwallis.

With this promising news in mind, Clinton left 10,000 British troops to hold New York and embarked in December on a stormy 38-day voyage south with 8,700 men. The destination was intended to be the patriot-held city of Charleston South Carolina but the fleet and its 90 transports was so damaged and scattered it had to first move south to Savannah to refit. At the fleet's arrival carrying such an imposing force patriot morale plummeted. Most of the American forces in the south were not regular "continental" soldiers but local militias and partisan bands whose willingness to fight was already low following the Savannah failure. Conversely, loyalist sentiment and activity increased and the situation took on the attributes of a civil war. Adding to the tribulations of the patriots was the arrival with Clinton's army of an obscure 26-year-old officer named Banastre Tarleton.

A RAPID RISE TO NOTORIETY

Tarleton was born into a wealthy Liverpool family and educated at Oxford University. After squandering most of the inheritance left to him by his father Tarleton used the remainder to buy a commission and joined the army in 1775. In the army he showed great aptitude as a dragoon officer and shortly after arriving in the colonies was given command of a "legion" that comprised most of the British cavalry in the southern colonies. As the name suggests, Tarleton's le-

gion contained both infantry and cavalry often supplemented with some light artillery. The American's had also organized some legions during the war. Tarleton's legion or, as it was properly known, "The British Legion" was first formed by Sir Henry Clinton in Philadelphia in 1778. In spite of the name, the legion was to be made up of Irish and other European volunteers but, when Tarleton took over as the acting commander, its ranks were filled primarily by American "provincials." These American legionnaires were familiar with the often-wild terrain and conditioned to the hot climate they were also familiar with the partisan tactics of their fellow countrymen and became very loyal to their new commander. The legion's cavalry operated as dragoons and wore green coats to distinguish them from the red coats of British regulars. At its peak Tarleton had about 450 men divided into 250 cavalry and 200 infantrymen. His legion joined Clinton's march north from Georgia into South Carolina in February 1780. The British had failed miserably in 1776 to take Charleston but, this time, the convergence of the army with the refitted British fleet allowed Clinton to conduct a protracted but successful siege resulting in the surrender of Lincoln and his army. This was Britain's most successful campaign in sometime and shortly after its conclusion a satisfied Clinton returned to his headquarters in New York leaving Cornwallis and the army to mop up the remaining rebel resistance in the Carolinas.

During the Charleston campaign Tarleton earned a reputation in the royal army as a capable light cavalry officer and anti-partisan leader. The stocky redheaded officer was also becoming both a hated and feared figure among the patriots. In the spring of 1780 Tarleton won three notable victories. The first on the 14th of April at the South Carolina crossroads town of Monck's Corner where, using information provided by a slave, Tarleton used his legion supported by some rangers to defeat a larger body of Continental Army cavalry. In the victory he acquired about 200 badly needed horses for the British and cut off any chance of Lincoln's army escaping the siege at Charleston. Following this, on May 6th Tarleton and his legion surprised the surviving American cavalry commanded by Abraham Buford at a ferry crossing on the Santee river. This fight at Lenud's Ferry cost the patriots a further 100 casualties many of whom drowned trying to swim the river and the loss of another 60 precious horses. The surrender of Lincoln's army at Charleston on May 12th left Buford's battered command as the only sizable patriot force in South Carolina.

Following the Charleston disaster Isaac Huger assumed command of the remaining patriots and ordered Buford to bring his cavalry north to Hillsborough North Carolina. Hearing of this move Clinton, before departing for New York, sent Cornwallis to intercept these remnants and c capture the now fugitive South Carolina patriot governor John Rutledge accompanying them. Cornwallis, in turn, sent Tarleton ahead to find them which he did on May 29th at a place called the Waxhaws. Tarleton had pushed his men and horses to near exhaustion and was only able to send 270 men into action. Yet again he crushed the more numerous patriots by using psychological tricks and superior tactics. The luckless Buford and only a few of his men escaped. Survivors claimed an attempt to surrender by white flag was refused by Tarleton's men who wrongly thought their commander had been killed and that a massacre followed. Whatever actually occurred, the word went out to patriots that no quarter had been given. Tarleton received the sobriquet "bloody Ban" and the killing of surrendering men became known as "Tarleton's quarter."

Tarleton's successes won him the full confidence of Lord Cornwallis who recognized a natural leader of shock troops. However, among other officers of the Royal Army there was much jealousy regarding his rapid rise to prominence. There was some good reason for this. Tarleton had so far been very lucky and he was arrogant, as one historian points out he was "cold-hearted, vindictive and utterly ruthless."

These characteristics were all on display at the Waxhaws. In the weeks that followed Tarleton was sent to suppress the partisan bands led by Francis Marion "The Swamp Fox" and Thomas Sumter known as "The Gamecock." Tarleton's luck held out when he became too sick with fever to accompany the British force that was destroyed by patriot "over the mountain men" at the Battle of King's Mountain. But the still recovering Tarleton was eluded by the Swamp Fox and fought to a standstill by The Gamecock in November 1780. Desperate to retrieve the bad situation in the south, the Continental Congress appointed General Horatio Gates to form a new patriot army in the Carolinas. As the commander of the Americans at the Battle of Saratoga in 1777, Gates was hailed as a hero. In reality Saratoga had been won by the efforts of Benedict Arnold and Daniel Morgan and Gates had shown little but a knack for scheming since. The overmatched Gates

and his army were easily defeated by Cornwallis at the Battle of Camden on August 16th. Cornwallis' obvious choice to lead the pursuit of Gates' shattered army was Tarleton who also finally caught up with Sumter who was covering the American retreat and this time destroyed the gamecock's command at the Battle of Fishing Creek on August 18th.

NEW LEADERS AND A NEW AMERICAN STRATEGY

Gates was accused of fleeing the battlefield at Camden and deserting the army. With his reputation in tatters, the American Continental Congress replaced him with Major General Nathanael Greene. The army that Greene took charge of included a new officer in its upper ranks, Daniel Morgan had recently arrived from Virginia.

Morgan was in most ways an exact opposite of the aristocratic Tarleton. The exact location in Southern New Jersey where Morgan was born in 1736 is unknown. His family was of Welsh descent and had a farm. At 17 the pugnacious Morgan left his family after a fight with his father and traveled southward into the Shenandoah valley of the Virginia colony. In 1755, at the start of the Seven Year's war, Morgan was working as a teamster and, in this capacity, joined the Army of English General Edward Braddock in 1757. Braddock's army that also included the young George Washington, was ambushed near the modern-day city of Pittsburgh and routed by the French and their Indian allies. Morgan was afterwards commended for his bravery in evacuating many of the wounded. However, the following year, the tall prideful Morgan slapped a British officer and received 500 lashes, a number that would have killed a lesser man. He was back in the fight in 1758 when an Indian's musket ball struck him in the neck passing out

with the American victory at Saratoga in 1777. Morgan played a leading role in this battle but when he was not promoted to general, his prideful nature led him to resign from the Army. George Washington who was a good judge of talent wanted Morgan back and in 1780 he convinced the congress to call for him to return. At first Morgan refused but when word of the failing patriot cause in the south reached him, he placed patriotism over pride and went south.

through his cheek and carrying away many of his teeth. The wound left a permanent hole in his cheek that was said to produce a whistling sound when he became excited and shouted!
In 1775 when the revolution began Morgan took command of a Virginia rifle company. He accompanied the American army that unsuccessfully invaded Canada where he showed great courage but was captured remaining a British prisoner for a year. On his release Morgan was made a Colonel and sent by George Washington to help halt the British invasion moving south into the New York colony which ended

At the time Morgan reached General Gates, the disgraced general was in the last days of holding command.
Gates had organized a new unit of light infantry that he turned over to Morgan. Congress also promoted him to Brigadier General. The light infantrymen were delighted with their tough, profane, and hard drinking leader. They called him "the Old Waggoneer" and prepared themselves for hard campaigning. Upon taking charge of the army, Greene detached Morgan with a 1000 man force. Greene's orders to Morgan were to move west and annoy the British who had established posts far inland, to secure supplies while denying them to the enemy, and to raise patriot morale by suppressing the back-country Loyalists. With these instructions in mind, Morgan left Greene with the main body of the army and marched west crossing the Catawba river.

THE CHASE INTO THE "BACK COUNTRY"

When Cornwallis discovered that Morgan was operating 200 kilometers away from the main patriot army and doing damage to his western flank he reacted quickly. The British commander feared that Morgan intended to attack the principle British post in the hinterlands, a fortified post called "Ninety-Six." When Cornwallis received word that Morgan's cavalry had massacred a sizable Loyalist militia unit in an action resembling the brutality of the Waxhaws, he turned to Tarleton who proposed taking his legion and some supporting troops west to attempt to cut off and destroy Morgan's command. Cornwallis would follow Tarleton with the bulk of the British army to close any possible patriot line of retreat.

Setting out from Winnsboro South Carolina on January 1st 1781 Tarleton led a well-equipped brigade which included his legion, 50 additional British dragoons, 200 men of the 7th regiment, 335 highlanders of the 71st regiment that included their light infantry company, a further two light infantry companies detached from other regiments and a Royal Artillery contingent with two 3 pound "grasshopper' field guns. This was a small but very good strike force and Tarleton was extremely confident that this force alone could destroy Morgan's command. Like most of the British leadership, Tarleton remained scornful of the patriot's fighting qualities. This was a mistake. Morgan's little army included excellent continental infantry from Maryland commanded by the experienced Colonel John Howard, continental dragoons led by William Washington, the cousin of George Washington, Morgan's North Carolina riflemen, militiamen from Georgia, South Carolina, and Virginia and some battle-tested partisans. Although Morgan worried that the militia units were not reliable in a pitched battle, this was a tough and experienced patriot force.

After covering over 120 kilometers over desolate and muddy roads, Tarleton located the patriots on January 15th. The search had worn down his army. Food was scarce and the British had none during the last forty-eight hours of the chase. Morgan had been retreating northwards attempting to avoid battle and was resting his men in an area known as the Cowpens. This was a region of rolling country comprised of woods of leafless trees in January and open pasture land where cattle were gathered before being driven to market. Morgan's scouts came in reporting Tarleton to be only eight kilometers away. They also inflated the size of the British force. Morgan continued to doubt that his militia would stand against the feared "Bloody Ban" Tarleton. The "old Waggoneer" also was concerned that he lacked artillery and sufficient cavalry. Like it or not, he had no choice but to fight as his line of retreat was blocked by the rain swollen Broad River. What Morgan did not know was that Tarleton's force was hungry and exhausted.

PREPARATION FOR BATTLE
Morgan elected to fight on the open ground of Cowpens he said later, because he didn't want the militia to have place to run and hide. Most of the patriot militia had arrived on horseback and the general feared they would panic and ride away. Morgan underestimated his militia. They were well-led and many were veterans of the Continental Army. In any case, Morgan selected a hill, bisected by the road leading back to the broad river, of about 400 meters in length to make his stand. The slope of the hill rose to a crest of about 30 meters behind which was a depression and then a second slope and crest of roughly the same height as the first about 600 meters behind the first. Beyond the second hill was a gully where Morgan posted his cavalry as a reserve. Morgan planned to deploy 150 of his best militia sharpshooters as skirmishers in a first line and 150 meters behind them the remainder of his militia under the command of the noted partisan Andrew Pickens. Howard with his 300 continentals formed a third line about 150 meters behind the militia just short of the hill's crest. Morgan's officers expressed concern about the flanks being largely unprotected, however Morgan dismissed their fears as his study of Tarleton's previous battles convinced him that the impetuous Tarleton would attack frontally. If Morgan had misgivings about the impending battle, he did not show them to his men. Many stories were later told about how the old waggoneer spent the entire night before the battle walking through the patriot camp, making certain that hot food was issued, cheering his men up by displaying his legendary lash scars, and challenging his militia marksmen to stand firm and deliver two volleys before falling back on the second line. This militia was composed of backcountry men like himself and Morgan knew how to motivate them. He reminded the militia of the second line to hold their fire until the British were "in killing distance" and to target their "epaulette men" meaning the officers. This display of humility and bravado did much to steady the nerves of his men and added greatly to his legend. What his men did not know was that Morgan was hiding from them the fact that he was in severe pain. The hard life Morgan had led left him suffering from rheumatism and other maladies.

The ever-aggressive Tarleton was inpatient on the eve of battle and in his eagerness gave his exhausted and starving men little time to rest. He broke camp at 3 in the morning leaving his baggage wagons behind and led by tory guides, pressed through the darkness for

8 kilometers, crossing a small stream and arriving before dawn with about 1.100 men. He quickly formed them up at the edge of a wood lying at the base of the patriot-held slope about 400 meters from the screen of patriot militia skirmishers and sent out scouts into the darkness to assess the position of the first American line. Beyond this the impetuous and over confident Tarleton did nothing to reconnaissance the ground and made no attempt to consult his older, more experienced officers or, to make contact with Lord Cornwallis' main army.

THE DAY OF BATTLE

As soon as the loyalist scouts reported the position of the patriot line at about 6:45, Tarleton launched his first attack using the 50 dragoons of the 17th regiment. It was cold and dawn was just breaking. The militia held their ground and delivered the promised two volleys emptying 15 saddles and sending the dragoons reeling back under the covering fire of the two British grasshopper cannons that blasted grapeshot at the militia sharpshooters falling back as planned on the second line. Seeing the patriot skirmish line appearing to break, Tarleton ordered his infantry to drop their packs, fix bayonets, and form two lines. Just as Morgan had suspected, Tarleton intended to attack the Americans head-on.

The British line was organized with 150 light infantrymen on the right supported on their left by one of the grasshopper cannons. The infantry of Tarleton's legion formed the center and the 200 men of the 7th regiment formed the left. The second grasshopper was placed between the 7th and the legionaries. The highlanders of the 71st were deployed as a second line about 150 meters behind the first and, because the British flanks were also "in the air" on the largely open slope, the remaining British dragoons were placed to the right of the light infantry and another 50 of Tarleton's dragoons were deployed to overlap the left. Tarleton's reserve was formed by the remainder of the dreaded legion cavalry.

At 7 o'clock the British line began its advance up the gentle slope with colors uncased and drums beating. The militia line commanded by Andrew Pickens and reinforced by the riflemen of the first line held their fire as Morgan had directed even when some panicky recruits of the 7th regiment began to fire. British officers quickly stopped this ineffective fire while maintaining the steady advance. Pickens gave the militia the order to fire at 100 meters. This was the "killing range" that Morgan had asked for. The volley yielded devastating results. Back country marksmanship was accurate and the attack wavered for a moment as about 40% of those struck down were officers and sergeants. British discipline was good and after a moment of confusion the advance continued. As planned Pickens' men fired a second but less effective volley and began to fall back in good order towards the American left flank. This appeared to Tarleton to be the expected rout and he ordered the remaining dragoons on his right to charge the militia. The cavalry charge did break the militia that began to flee in disorder toward the safety of the third patriot line and in the direction of their horses tethered nearby. This was a moment of crisis for the Americans and only the efforts of Pickens and an officer "of remarkable fleetness of foot" named Hughes stopped them from disappearing.

As the dragoons with sabers drawn approached the wavering mass of patriot militia, they received a volley from a body of Virginia riflemen and then were struck by a counter charge of William Washington's continental dragoons. The British cavalry was shocked by the sudden appearance of the previously concealed American cavalry and recoiled leaving at least 10 dead behind them.

After seeing off the dragoons of the 17th regiment, Washington and his men returned to the protection provided by the rear of the second hill and rested their horses.

It was now 7:45 and Tarleton still believed that the rout of the Americans was imminent. Reforming his infantry, he resumed his attack focusing on the third Patriot line comprised of Howard's continentals. This brought on an intense fire fight between the two lines resulting in what Tarleton later recalled as "great slaughter." The intense fire slowed but did not halt the British advance. As the struggle continued, Tarleton rode over to the commander of the Highlanders, Major MacArthur and ordered him to turn the exposed American right flank.

MacArthur later claimed that he was also told to take no prisoners. The 71st was Tarleton's largest infantry unit and its men were some of the best and most experienced troops in the British southern army. They came on at the Americans ascending the highest part of the slope with bayonets leveled and their bag pipes playing a march. Howard was a cool and experienced soldier and seeing this new threat ordered his left to fall back and face the Highlanders. This maneuver known as "refusing the flank" involved a pivot and was difficult to perform especially while an attack was in progress and, in the confusion, the other men in Howard's battleline thought a general withdrawal was underway. The continentals began retiring up the slope in good order, but this was not the plan and Morgan rode over to confront Howard. Neither man could safely halt the withdrawal at that point so Morgan told Howard to fall back some distance and try to reform his command.

Seeing the backs of their enemies and, missing many officers and sergeants, the British lost their discipline and their bayonet attack lost cohesion. The shouting British soldiers followed the patriot line disappearing over the crest of the first hill and chased them over. William Washington was on the American left with his cavalry and saw the situation that was developing. He sent word to General Morgan that he could see the British advancing "like a mob" and if Howard's continentals could stop and deliver a volley Washington would swing around the American rear and attack the British in the flank. When Morgan received this message, he called to Howard to stop the withdrawal and reform. The American infantry who were skilled at reloading their muskets while on the move obeyed this command and stopped a few meters up the second slope hurriedly reforming a firing line. The British attack was only ten meters away when the patriots delivered their volley that staggered the British and then counter attacked with their bayonets. This was enough for the winded British fusiliers, legion and light infantry. Most surrendered and a few fled off toward the American left. Some Ame-

The battle of Cowpens
Juanuary 17 1781

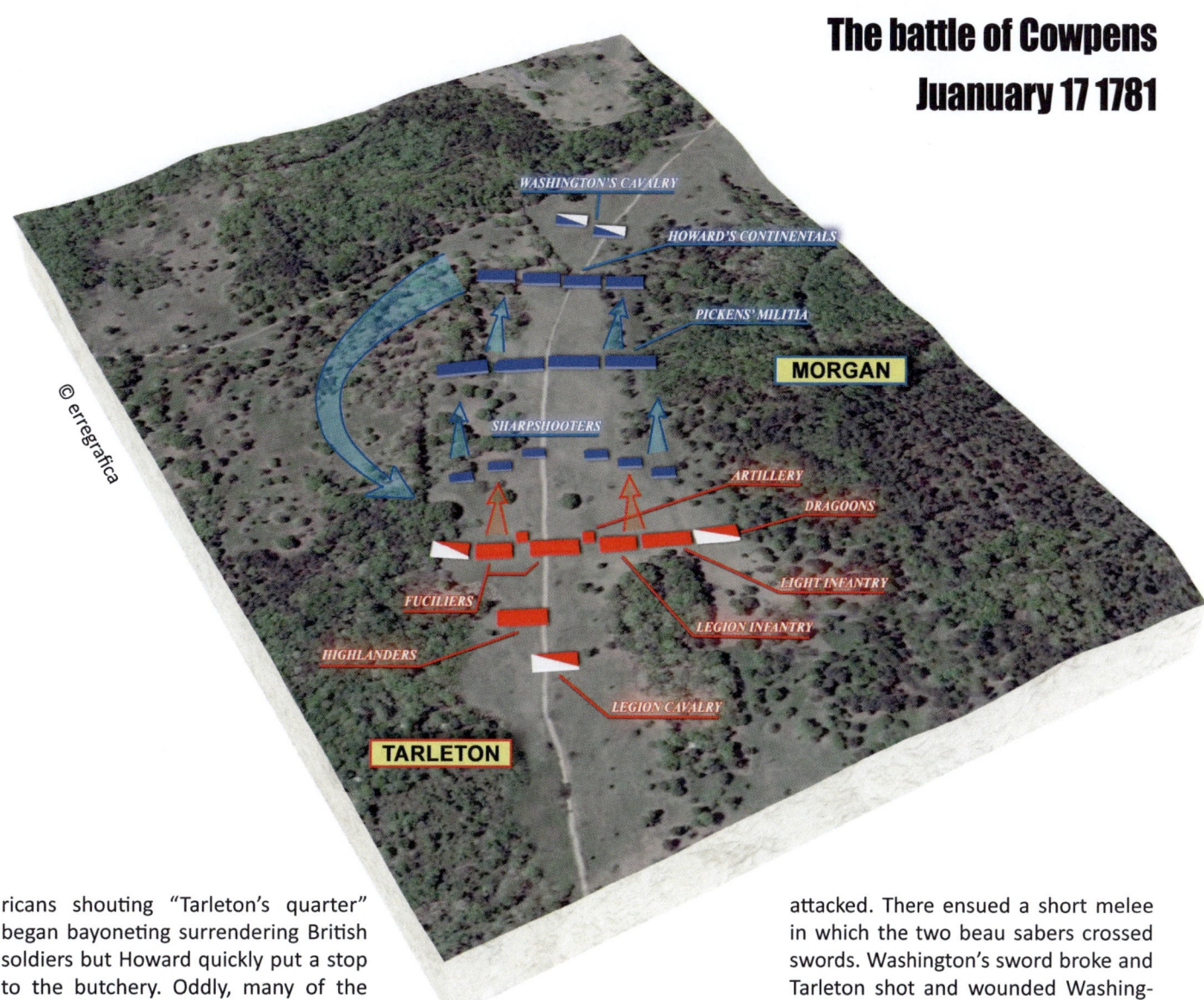

ricans shouting "Tarleton's quarter" began bayoneting surrendering British soldiers but Howard quickly put a stop to the butchery. Oddly, many of the surrendering British simply lay down on the ground. This may be an indication of how exhausted and hungry they were.

Tarleton tried desperately to rally the men and sent for his 200-legion dragoons in reserve to charge in support of the crumbling British infantry. When they refused to respond to their officer's orders, Tarleton started to ride back to personally rally them but his horse was killed. The veteran infantry of the 71st continued fighting until they were attacked from three sides. Washington's Cavalry struck their left while the American militia under Pickens recovered their nerve and joined in the attack on the right. With their fate sealed, MacArthur called for his survivors to lay down their arms.

Meanwhile other Americans overran the two grasshopper guns that had advanced with the British infantry. All of the gunners were killed or captured. Tarleton after being given another horse charged the guns with the fifty legion cavalrymen stationed on the left flank in an attempt to recapture them but veered off when the patriots turned the cannons around to face him. At that moment William Washington and his patriot cavalry spotted Tarleton and attacked. There ensued a short melee in which the two beau sabers crossed swords. Washington's sword broke and Tarleton shot and wounded Washington's horse before racing off to safety. This dramatic moment concluded the battle.

The retreating British Legion cavalry discovered that the teamsters had cut the horse's traces pulling their baggage wagons and ridden off while the men of the loyalist militia were found looting the wagon's contents and cut down by Tarleton's outraged dragoons. The rest of the baggage was dragged from the wagons and burned. That night Tarleton forced a local farmer at gun point to guide them to safety. Tarleton with about 200 surviving dragoons rode 25 miles to find Lord Cornwallis' camp arriving on the 18th.

The losses to British amounted to 87% of their available forces. These troops were some of the finest soldiers of Cornwallis' army. It is said that when Tarleton reported to Cornwallis conveying word of the disaster the British general leaned so hard upon his sword that it broke. The best of Cornwallis' army was gone. The British general told his second in command Lord Rawdon that "the late affair has almost broke my heart." Particularly painful was the loss of his light infantry. Although a few escaped, the infantry of the British legion was destroyed as a fighting force. While exact numbers are disputed, it is believed that the British lost 110 dead, a very high proportion of them officers. In addition, about 825 prisoners were taken along with 800 muskets, two cannons, 100 horses and 35 wagons. The Americans also helped themselves to the prisoner's personal belongings. Morgan's army suffered about 100 casualties.

The lasting results of this battle of envelopment, a sort of Cannae in a cow pasture, were that Cornwallis had to continue his southern campaign in a seriously weakened condition. The Americans on the other hand, had learned how to use their militia and Morgan's tactic of placing them in the front as a skirmish line was repeated by Greene at the Battle of Guilford's courthouse in March of that year.

Tarleton was undeniably brave and inspirational as a leader of cavalry but, his arrogance led him to underestimate his opponent. Tarleton had attacked a rested army with one that was exhausted and Hungry and he had done so without properly surveying the ground. In a more perfect world, perhaps one imagined by certain Australian actors, Tarleton would have been killed or, at least ruined by this debacle. Instead, Cornwallis, exonerated his favorite cavalryman in the face of harsh criticism by other British officers. Tarleton and the remainder of his legion continued to serve Cornwallis effectively as raiders and scouts until the British southern army was cornered and forced to surrender at Yorktown Virginia in October 1781. Returning to England after the war Tarleton was promoted to general but never received another command. He served without distinction in Parliament and gained a reputation as a womanizer. Daniel Morgan was hailed by his countrymen as a hero. Unlike

Tarleton, Morgan's tactics were conceived from an understanding of his men, their backcountry pride and their abilities. Cowpens was the end of Morgan's service in America's Revolutionary war. Suffering badly from his many wounds and rheumatism, he again left the army and retired to his Virginia farm. Like Tarleton he later gravitated toward politics where he used his status as a hero and people skills to be elected to the House of Representatives. He died on his Virginia farm in 1802.

ORDER OF BATTLE
Should you wish to try to beat Tarleton yourself, here is an order of Battle.

THE AMERICAN ARMY*
Commander: Brigadier General Daniel Morgan
"Continental Army" forces
Lieutenant Colonel John Howard
Maryland Line 3 companies - Veteran 180 men
Virginia company - Veteran 60 men
N. Carolina company - Veteran 307 men
Delaware company - Veteran 60 men
Lieutenant Colonel William Washington
Virginia Cavalry - Veteran 80 men
Virginia Militia - Green 100 men
Colonel Andrew Pickens
Georgia, North Carolina and South Carolina militia - Green 490 men
Lieutenant Col. James McCall
Georgia and South Carolina Militia mounted infantry - Green 45 men
* My total is 1,322 but American numbers are still disputed and may have numbered as many as 1600
Note: Most Patriot militia were armed with muskets but, the 150 men of the first line were armed primarily with rifles.

THE BRITISH ARMY
Commander: Lieutenant Colonel Banastre Tarleton
7th Regiment of Foot - Major Timothy Newmarsh - Green 200 men
71st Regiment of Foot Highlanders 1st Battalion - Major Archibald McArthur - Veteran 335 men
Infantry of The British Legion - Veteran 250 men
16th Regiment's light infantry company - Veteran 50 men
Prince of Wales Loyalist Regt - Good 50 men
17th regiment of Dragoons - Veteran 50 men
Dragoons of the British Legion* - Veteran 250 men
Royal Artillery two 3 pound "grasshoppers"- Veteran 50 men
The British total of 1,235 excludes the Loyalist militia with the baggage.
*Legion cavalry should be considered elite under Tarleton's personal command.

WARGAMING WITH BASIC BATTLES
There are several specific rules to play the American War of Independence. If you don't have a reference rulebook and are looking for so-

mething simple and affordable, we suggest Basic Battles, the "Age of the Musket" expansion of our Basic Impetus rules. It is a free to download pdf available through Wargames Vault that will turn soon into a complete rulebook. These are the orders of battle for Basic Battles to game the Battle of Cowpens.

AMERICANS
Line 3xFT VBU=5, I=2, VD=2, Musket C, Veterans
Line 1xFT VBU=5, I=2, VD=2, Musket C, Recruits
Virginia Cavalry 1xCL VBU=3, I=2, VD=1, Veterans
Skirmishing Militia 3xS VBU=2, I=1, VD=1, Musket C, Green
Riflemen 4xS VBU=2, I=0, VD=1, Musket B

BRITISH
71st Highlanders 1xFT VBU=6, I=3, VD=3, Musket C, Elite
7th Infantry 1xFT VBU=6, I=2, VD=3, Musket C, Recruits
British Legion Inf. 1xFT VBU=6, I=2, VD=3, Musket C, Veterans
16th Light Infantry Company 1xS VBU=3, I=1, VD=1, Musket C
Loyalists 1xFT VBU=4, I=1, VD=1, Musket C, Recruits
17th Dragoons 1xCL VBU=3, I=2, VD=1
British Legion Dragoons 1xCL VBU=4, I=2, VD=2, Elite
Artillery 1xArt VBU=1, I=0, VD=1, Art B

THE ROMAN ARMY
FROM SEPTIMIUS SEVERUS TO CONSTANTINE

by MARCO ORTALDA

Over the centuries the Roman Empire extended its holdings over the entire Mediterranean or, as some Emperors preferred to view it, over the entire civilized world. As the Julio-Claudian and Flavian dynasties consolidated and expanded the Empire, the imperial adoption method of the second century yielded positive results. Ironically, it was the philosopher Emperor Marcus Aurelius who interrupted this system by placing his own son on the throne: the unfit Commodus.

When Septimius Severus, legate of Pannonia in command of the powerful Danubian legions, marched on Rome proclaiming himself emperor, he did not think he would in turn create yet another method. If a legate could threaten power and become Emperor why could not other commanders of equal rank do so? Septimius Severus was the first to adopt for himself the title of Augustus and for his successors that of Caesar. His sons Geta and Caracalla failed to establish a joint dynasty as their father had hoped. In 217, Caracalla was killed by a praetorian prefect, Macrinus, whose reign lasted less than a year and a half. In the time between the natural death of Septimius Severus in 211 and Diocletian's accession to the throne in 284, there were to be twenty-four emperors and an even greater number of usurpers. Except for a few rare cases (Claudius II died of plague, Valerian was taken prisoner by the Sassanids) all reigned a few years and died violent deaths.

Continued internal struggles were accompanied by a continual change in the enemies faced by Rome. As early as the 2nd century, the peoples on the Rhine and Danube, once divided into the countless tribes illustrated by Tacitus in his "Germania," had taken advantage of the Empire's turmoil to create vast federations. The Franks, Alemanni and Saxons in the 3rd century concentrated much larger contingents than the Hermundurians, Usipetians, Catti etc. Probably it was the Roman presence on the borders, together with Rome's continual penetrations into their territory, that was the main influence in the attempt to unite the various tribes.

28mm miniatures from Gripping Beast, Warlord Games, A&A. Marco Ortalda collection.

A slinger discuss with a Roman officer

By 224, in the East, the Parthian or Arsacid dynasty had given way to the more aggressive Sassanid dynasty. However, if one could reach back in time and interview a Roman emperor, he would surely be stunned to hear that the shattering of the Empire occurred not because of the Persian threat but because of the invasions of the Germanic peoples. This is because throughout the second century, and even more so in the third and fourth, every Emperor worth his salt considered the Parthians first and later the Sassanids the only serious enemy of Rome.

All these elements lead to a major change in the army structure of the empire. A widely held view is that this period is one characterized by moral, political, and military decadence, as a kind of prelude to the Dark Ages. In fact, there is no evidence to say that the army had considerably reduced its efficiency.

Rome's enemies, sensing the Empire's internal difficulties, caused a need to constantly reinforce the limes from attacks by raising military expenditures. The increasing tax burden, the devastation associated with enemy raids, and the depopulation of entire border regions caused the devaluation of Roman money.

As can be well understood, the Goths, Franks, Alemanni, Saxons, and Sassanids were adversaries capable of significant offensive actions, and, continuing internal struggles forced the Romans to change their strategy. Losing the initiative, their actions became more reactive rather than aimed at further conquest. Moreover, an extended front from Britain to the Euphrates required many soldiers and significant mobility to deal with threats at multiple points, often at the same time.

The strategy of twenty-five or thirty legions stationed at strategic points along the border could no longer be followed. The idea of being able to move entire legions or parts of them (*vexillationes*), thus disengaging from an entire area, was no longer sufficient because of the increased fear of enemy incursions or the risk of elevating a new potential usurper.

THE CHANGE OF STRATEGY IN THE 3RD CENTURY

In a piecemeal fashion, during the 3rd century, due to the constant changes of emperors, a system of elastic defense was adopted. A strategy in depth based on mobile field units became necessary in case the defenses were broken through at a certain point.

During the 1st and 2nd centuries the existance of the Praetorians and Germans of the custodes corps did not represent a true reserve army. Somewhat forcibly, it can be argued that Septimius Severus' decision to station the 2nd legio Parthica at Albano reflected, on the one hand, the emperor's need for a

Eastern Roman archers

strong contingent to keep the center of power in check but, also, an early embryonic strategic reserve.

In addition to the idea of a "reserve" or "maneuver" army, a new system of fortifications began to develop during the 3rd century. More massive strongholds were built at strategic points some even well within imperial territory.

In the 3rd century a system of defense in depth began to develop. In 270 Aurelian ordered the building of a new wall around Rome. Thus, we begin to see the creation of fortified cities, granaries, and villas capable of withstanding long sieges against enemies lacking siege tools. Many Roman victories thus became logistical victories. The presence of fortifications that were difficult to conquer and forced the "barbarians" to retreat due to the lack of provisions, or because of the arrival of fresh reinforcement troops.

It was during this period that multi-provincial military districts were created with a clear separation of military and civil power. The posts of *dux ripae* of Dura Europos, the *corrector orientalis* entrusted to Marcellinus by Aurelian, and other such commands fall within this framework. This arose from the need to place a person trusted by the emperor in the areas where enemies could penetrate. In this system the defensive reaction would be faster. The idea of a defensive army on the borders and a "reserve" army that could intervene in case of difficulty was implemented.

The nature of the commands also changed. During the Julio-Claudian dynasty, the governors of strategic provinces where troops were stationed and the command of the legion itself were entrusted to men of the senatorial class (*legatus augusti legionis*). The backbone of the legion, however, from the *primipilus* to the *tribunus laticlavious*, was filled by those of the equestrian class. In the 3rd century, when it became necessary to detach part of the

A ballista ready to fire

legionary cohorts to form a *vexillationes*, the command was often given to a knight rather than a senator. In this period, moreover, precisely to prevent an entire area from being left unattended, *vexillationes* became something of a custom. Very often these detached units after repelling the enemy did not return to the legion of origin, becoming independent units themselves.

This is the backdrop which gave rise to power of the Illyrian emperor-soldiers such as Diocletian and the creation of independent commands such as the *dux ripae* were framed, which saw for the first time a detachment between civil power, formerly entrusted to the governor, and military power. The new duces, reported in the *Notitia Dignitatum*, professional soldiers of equestrian origin who controlled a diverse set of units scattered throughout the territory, no longer a single legion.

THE REFORM OF GALLIENUS (260-268 CE)

In 260 Publius Licinius Ignatius Gallienus became emperor, prematurely. The son of Emperor Valerian, this young man was forced to become emperor when his father was defeated and captured by the Sassanids. Gallienus is usually credited with a reform of the army through the creation of an early "army of maneuver" quartered within the empire rather than on its borders. These were mobile cavalry units stationed in Milan that could intervene when needed It must be pointed out that although cavalry began to assume an important role in this period in terms of numbers, the queen of battles continued to be infantry. What is important to note is that cavalry soldiers assumed a new status similar to that of the comitatus of Diocletian and Constantine. Not surprisingly, two emperors, Claudius II and Aurelian, rose to the highest office precisely because of their good record as commanders of these troops. In addition to the cavalry stationed in Milan, Gallienus set up other mobile units at Poetovio (present-day Ptuj in Slovenia), Sirmium (Sirmio in Serbia) and Lychidnos (in Greece). Some authors consider these detachments another example of maneuver armies.

Others, however, see them as a simple strategic response to the abandonment of the *Agri decumates* (territories between the Rhine and Danube) that had brought the threat of invasions closer to central power. In any case, it is undeniable that, with Gallienus, we begin to see a defensive system based on a maneuver army placed in the rear.

DIOCLETIAN'S REFORM (284-330 CE)

In 284 a Roman general of humble origins who had worked his way up in the army from the position of a simple legionnaire became emperor: Diocles or, as he is better known, Gaius Aurelius Valerius Diocletian.

Defending the limes

The history of Diocletian's life alone could be the subject of an article. In fact, in all history books Diocletian is remembered for being the one who reorganized the Empire by dividing it into two parts: a western and an eastern part. Diocletian positioned his comrade in arms Maximian as a co-emperor also creating the premise for a succession system. Diocletian and Maximian, while both assuming the office of emperor were not placed on the same level. The Augustus Iovus Diocletian (protected by Jupiter) was assisted by his second Augustus Herculius (protected by the semi-god Hercules) to whom he entrusted the western part of the Empire. The two parts were further divided into two districts entrusted to two Caesars, the designated successors. The empire became a tetrarchy with four capitals: Milan and Trier in the West, and Sirmio and Nicomedia in the East.

The social reform of the Empire is quite complex, but what interests us at this juncture is that it is accompanied by military reform. Each Augustus/Cesar had his own autonomous units, a kind of *comitatus*, to be used in the event of border breakthroughs. The army was increased in numbers and troops were better distributed along the borders. We begin to glimpse the difference between *limitanee* troops (static border garrisons) and *comitatus* (maneuver units). In addition, there was a strengthening of the defensive system. The fortresses of this period, either built from scratch or rebuilt, had thicker walls and towers that were no longer square but round to facilitate defense. Diocletian's goal was to provide the Empire with a first layer of defense held by limited troops supported by fortified installations in the interior capable of withstanding sieges, and if necessary, a maneuver army commanded by the Augustus/Cesar on duty capable of intervening. Thus, there was a shift from a "linear" defensive system to a complex of fortresses and garrisons inside the empire that allowed for defense in depth.

With Diocletian we also see the consolidation of the idea of autonomous military districts controlled by a *dux provinciae* or *dux limitis*. Diocletian as a career military man of humble origins appointed experienced soldiers of the equestrian order as duces, relegating the Senate and its class, to a secondary position.

I would like to point out that the limitanean troops did not compose a second "class" army. During the 3rd century traditional Roman legions were often divided into *vexillationes* sent to distant places. After completing their task these *vexillationes* were supposed to return "home" but, very often, they remain in their new place of destination. Diocletian's limitanean troops often included what remained of ancient legions while *vexillationes* that were often far from their base legion, assumed the rank of independent units themselves.

As we know, the system of succession devised by Diocletian declined while its author was still alive but, not the new way of conceiving of the defense of the Empire that would be perfected by another great general: Constantine.

CONSTANTINE'S REFORM (306 - 337 CE)

With Diocletian the idea of a mobile army composed around the *comitatus*, i.e., wards that moved together with the Agustus or Caesar, became established. With the arrival of Constantine in 324, the evolution of the late imperial

Cataphracts charging

system was completed by the creation of a permanent mobile army. The imperium of Constantine I, even more than that of Diocletian, represented a revolution of the social and military systems of the Late Empire. He moved the capital from Rome to Byzantium and dissolved the Praetorian Guard that had protected the emperors for three hundred years. Together with Licinius, he issued the Edict of Milan establishing freedom of worship, and many other reforms.

In the military aspect, Constantine created a new army with two types of troops: Mobile troops (*comitatenses*) flanked by palatinee units (elite cavalry following the emperor who had replaced the praetorians) and *pseudocomitatenses* troops: originally *limitanee* units assigned to mobile armies.

The division between comitatenses, palatinae, and pseudocomitatenses had more to do with rank and salary than of actual military function.

Fortunately, we have valuable sources during this period such as the *Notitia Dignitatum*, an anonymous document listing the major military and civil units of the 4th century, and the *Res gestae* of Ammianus Marcellinus, a historical text written by a career military man describing the events of the Empire from Nerva to Valens.

In the *Notitia Dignitatum* the term legiones is often given alongside various units. Constantine further increased the army's numbers above the increase already made by Diocletian even though the legions of the late empire were numerically smaller than those of Augustus. A legion *comitatensis* could probably field between 1,000 and 1,500 soldiers. Alongside these units were the *Auxilia*. The armament and organization of the auxiliary soldiers compared to the legionaries were similar. Probably, the *Auxilia* were introduced as light infantry to flank the heavy legionary infantry, but this division is not always clear. Again, this was probably a difference in rank rather than actual military function.

The names of the new units referred to cities, peoples or their specialization. If the imperial legions of the Julio-Claudian dynasty were called such names as legio Italica, XX Valeria, XII Fulminata, XVI Flavia and so on, the new legions were named such things as l*ovinai seniores*, *Batavi seniores*, *Equites scutarii Illyriciani*, *Lanciarii Gallicani Honoriani* etc.

Unlike the *limitanei*, the *comitatenses* troops did not have a fixed base but were moved as needed while waiting to undertake any military action planned by their officers.

The *limitanei* or *ripenses* (if troops stationed near a river border) were units firmly rooted to the territory. Having created an army of maneuver, the use of *vexillationes* was reduced and the *limitanei* were allowed to remain in their original destinations. This in part reinforced the idea of the limitanei soldiers as soldier-peasants. In fact, at least throughout the 4th century and part of the 5th, the border troops were adequately trained. So much so that some of these units were aggregated with the armies of maneuver, taking on the name *pseudocomitatenses* in the *Notitia*.

The last aspect to note concerns the military hierarchies. The tribunes and legates represented the highest ranks in the early Empire but the figure of the magister became established in the 3rd century. Constantine devised two positions in command of the mobile army: the *magister peditum* and the *magister equitum*. As the name suggests, the former was an infantry commander while the latter was a cavalry commander. This subdivision of command was certainly in keeping with the traditions of the Roman republican army, but it also prevented one charismatic commander from having control of the entire army. In the 4th century, based on the *Notitia Dignitatum*, the figure of the magister was extended to regional mobile armies such as the *magister peditum* per Gallias or Illyricum, per Orientem etc. The *Duces*, between the 4th and 5th centuries, also experienced an evolution by becoming military commanders of limitanean troops. Initially, these *Duces* were figures with strictly military assignments, but with the weakening of central power they began to deal with enlistment and to assume the role of judge in cases of military matters.

CONCLUSIONS

We have seen how the system devised by Gallienus and refined by Diocletian and Constantine involved a series of fortifications at some distance from the borders and the formation of a maneuver army in response to systemic crises. This system could combine defence with short campaigns of conquest, but it was fundamentally a defensive system. The days of the feats of Julius Caesar, Octavian or Trajan were long gone. Only a great general like Constantine would be able to carry out successful military campaigns against the Goths. His dynasty would attempt to achieve its dream of conquering the Sassanid Empire but, Constantius II first then, Julian later, would die in the attempt. The former because of a fever that also averted yet another civil war, the latter because of betrayal by his own officers. Both found themselves on more than one occasion having to divert their forces from the objective to eliminate a usurper of the day.

Unfortunately, the size of the empire, political instability, and the end of major campaigns of conquest with their influx of large amounts of gold created the elements that would break down the Roman defensive system. Continuous influxes of men and resources were needed to ensure a defence in depth and to keep the fortifications efficient. Continued Germanic incursions further weakened the economy and caused the abandonment or depopulation of areas crucial to the Empire such as Gaul and Britain. Gradually the Western Empire unravelled by trying to come to terms with the newcomers and convincing itself that it had turned their holdings into client states. The barbarian Roman kingdoms of the 5th and 6th centuries contended only for the memory of Rome's greatness, as little by little they came to follow different paths.

NÖRDLINGEN 1634

by LORENZO SARTORI

To fully understand the significance and consequences of the Battle of Nördlingen, the last one fought by the Swedes during the 30 Years War, it is necessary to take a step back to when Gustavus Adolphus II of Sweden decided to enter the most destructive conflict fought in Europe up to that time.

SWEDEN IN THE 30 YEARS WAR

An ambitious man, with a military education imparted at a young age, Gustavus Adolphus ascended the Swedish throne in 1611 when his country was engaged in no less than three conflicts: against the Principality of Moscow (Ingria War, 1610-1617), against Denmark (Kalmar War 1611-1613) and against Poland (Polish-Swedish War 1610-1611). During the latter conflict, Gustavus Adolphus established an anti-Habsburg alliance with the German Protestant princes, since the Poles had formed an alliance with the Empire, the consequence of which was the conquest of Pomerania by Austrian troops. Thus, on 6 July 1630, under the pretext of championing the Protestant cause, but with the aim of extending his area of influence beyond the Baltic, the Swedish king landed on the island of Usedom in Pomerania at the head of a powerful and modern army: 30,000 infantrymen and 6,000 cavalrymen, many veterans and largely financed by Cardinal Richelieu's France, in the common interest of opposing Habsburg hegemony.

This began the so-called Swedish period of the Thirty Years' War (the previous Danish phase had ended in 1626 with the disastrous defeat of Christian IV of Denmark at the Battle of Lutter).

Although they were in favour of the Swedes, no Protestant prince at first supported Gustavus Adolphus' expedition.

Swedish. Horse (28mm Renegade) painted by Renato Genovese. Foot (28mm Warlord), painted by Guido Bogi. Imperials (28mm Warlord), painted by Gianluca Pinardi, collection Giorgio Ranieri.

He would have to win their active support with success in the field.

On 17 September 1631, the Scandinavian ruler, nicknamed the Lion of the North, defeated the Catholic troops led by the Count of Tilly at the Battle of Breitenfeld in Saxony. The linear tactics of the Swedish infantry immediately proved more effective than the traditional tercio, a deeper, more solid formation, but static and able to deliver a smaller volume of fire. The Swedish combined use of horsemen and musketeers also proved successful against the powerful Imperial cuirassiers. With the artillery the Swedes also imposed their superiority, inflicting a considerable number of losses at the start of the battle on the deep ranks of the tercios, which were very vulnerable to cannon fire.

The success at Breitenfed was reconfirmed at the Battle of Rain (15 April 1632) during the campaign to conquer Bavaria. Once again it was Tilly who was defeated, who in addition to the battle also lost his life as he was mortally wounded in the leg by a cannonball.

Gustavus Adolf's dream was shattered, however, at Lutzen on 16 November 1632. This time the Lion of the North had to reckon with Albrecht von Wallenstein who, recently returned from retirement and had already inflicted a first defeat on him at Alte Veste on 3 September. At Lutzen, Wallenstein arranged the imperial troops in defensive positions, in some cases entrenched, adopting slimmer infantry formations, more similar to those of his adversaries. The weak point of the imperial deployment, however, remained the left flank, formed by a few divisions of cuirassiers cleverly covered by Croatian light cavalry. It was there that Gustavus Adolphus decided to strike the enemy's deployment.

The initial success on that side of the front however, was stopped by the late arrival of Gottfried zu Pappenheim and his cavalry. The celebrated German general was, in the course of this counter attack, mortally wounded by musket fire. Meanwhile, on the left side of the Swedish line the situation remained essentially balanced. So, the Lion of the North decided to lead a cavalry charge to restore cohesion on the opposite wing. How it ended is well-known to history. Gustavus Adolphus was hit and unseated by two musket shots and surrounded by imperial foot soldiers. Instead of surrendering he is said to have shouted: "I am the King of Sweden, I seal the religion and freedom of the German Nation with my blood." He was finished off with pikes.

In the end, however, Wallenstein decided to retreat and leave the field to the Swedes. Lutzen thus remains the last victory of the Lion of the North, but the beginning of the end of the Swedish phase. And here we come to the battle of Noerdlinger, which marks the very end of this phase and, as we shall see, the Tercio's revenge.

THE AFTERMATH OF GUSTAVUS ADOLPHUS

With the death of Gustavus Adolphus, power passed into the hands of Axel Oxenstierna the Swedish Grand Chancellor while military leadership was entrusted to the ambitious and impulsive Bernard of Saxe-Weimar and the more cautious Gustav Horn, Marshal of Sweden. Despite the desire for peace expressed by many German states exhausted by the war, Oxenstierna did not seem willing to give way and on 18 March 1633 promoted the creation of the Heilbronn League, involving the princes of the Upper and Lower Rhine, Swabia and Franconia. France also increased its involvement in the war economically in favour of the Protestant cause. On the Catholic side Wallenstein, who had made his fortune from the war, at the expense of the imperial coffers, was more than ready to continue it.

Militarily, however, the war entered a period of stalemate, with sieges and cities being occupied and liberated, once by the Catholics, the next by the Protestants.

Meanwhile, another protagonist appeared on the scene: Spain. Until then, the involvement of the Spanish crown in the Thirty Years' War had been considered 'peripheral'. The Spanish had been engaged for decades in Flanders against the Netherlands and between 1628 and 1631 in northern Italy in the ill-fated war of succession of Mantua and Monferrato. They had never intervened directly in Germany, which was considered the central theatre of the conflict. After the rapid Swedish advance, Ferdinand II wrote several times to the court in Madrid proposing an alliance between Austria and Spain in an anti-Protestant alliance ignoring the fact that in 1625 the Spanish had made the same proposal that was not accepted by the empire. Previously, the Protestants to be confronted by Spain were those of the Netherlands, while for the Austrians it was those of Germany.

Sweden's entry into the war, the growing support of France (a thorn in the side for the Spanish) and above all the need to clear the 'Spanish Way', also known as the Flanders Corridor, i.e. the overland route that allowed Spanish troops to move from northern Italy to Flanders or vice versa, prompted Madrid to meet the emperor's call. The Spanish also hoped that, once the issue in Germany had been resolved, Ferdinand II would help them in Flanders.

The route known as the Spanish way was used for the first time in 1567, when the Tercio of Lombardy, Naples, Sicily and Sardinia, 10,000 men, under the command of the Duke of Alba, set off from Milan and reached Brussels in 56 days. From then until 1620, the Spa-

niards had passed more than 123,000 men along this land route, compared to less than 18,000 by sea, which was considered less safe.

However, in 1633 much of the Spanish route was under the control of Protestant or French troops. It was for that reason that a Spanish army, under the command of Gómez Suárez de Figueroa, fourth Duke of Feria, was deployed with the aim of securing the Rhine route and collaborating with the imperial troops. It was too bad that Feria found himself blocked by Wallenstein, who, jealous of the presence of another Catholic army on German soil, forbade the passage of Spanish troops into Alsace, creating a diplomatic incident between Madrid and Vienna. In the end, Ferdinand managed to impose himself on his general, granting passage to the 1,300 horsemen and 10,500 infantrymen of Feria.

On 8 July 1633, the Swedes defeated the Imperials on the field in Hessen at the Battle of Odelnorf.
On 1 October Feria joined a second imperial army in Ravensburg, led by Ferdinand of Hungary (future Ferdinand III) and Johann von Aldringen, a general who until a few weeks earlier had been in the service of Wallenstein. The Spanish-imperial army marched on Constance, forcing Horn to lift a siege, after which it took the towns of Waldshut, Laufenburg and Sackingen undisturbed.

As the Catholic army approached, the Swedes also laid siege to Breisach. Having lost control of the Rhine, Horn's troops set their sights on Bavaria, in particular on the fortress of Regensburg, crucial for the lines of communication with Austria.
Ferdinand II found himself having to beg Wallenstein to mobilise his army and received another refusal. By now the imperial general was fighting his own personal war and only out of self-interest decided a few days later to attack the Swedes and Saxons in Silesia, defeating them at the Battle of Steinau on the Oder River.
This victory did not prevent the Protestants from occupying Regensburg on 13 November, while a second Protestant army prepared to attack Bohemia. Ferdinand was forced to decide whether to defend Bohemia or Bavaria. He decided for Bavaria, as this would allow him to free the Danube corridor, as well as preserve his relationship with Catholic Bavaria.

In December 1633, once again the emperor was forced to put himself in the hands of the increasingly difficult Wallenstein who refused to mobilise the army during the winter. AS a result, Feria was forced to retreat and a typhus epidemic decimated the Spanish army.
 The duke also died during this time of typhus. Wallenstein, considered increasingly unreliable, was dismissed and the following month the commander was assassinated in a plot hatched by some of his own officers.

THE ROAD TO NÖRDLINGEN

Once the winter had passed, hostilities resumed on several fronts in the spring of 1634, but the greatest efforts were made by Horn who, between March and April, captured the towns of Biberach, Kempton and Memmingen, while another Protestant army, under Arnim's orders, defeated the imperial army at Colloredo in Silesia. In the meantime, Ferdinand of Hungary (who was to become emperor in 1637) was called in to replace Wallenstein, with General Matthias Gallas as second in command.

The imperialists could count on 15,000 infantrymen, 1,500 dragoons, 9,000 cavalrymen to which 3,000 Croatian light cavalrymen had to be added. They also have about 30 heavy artillery pieces, mortars and 116 light cannons. In Bavaria, there were also von Aldringen's troops (5,000 infantrymen, 3,000 cavalrymen and 600 Croats), the Bavarian army (4,500 infantrymen, 3,000

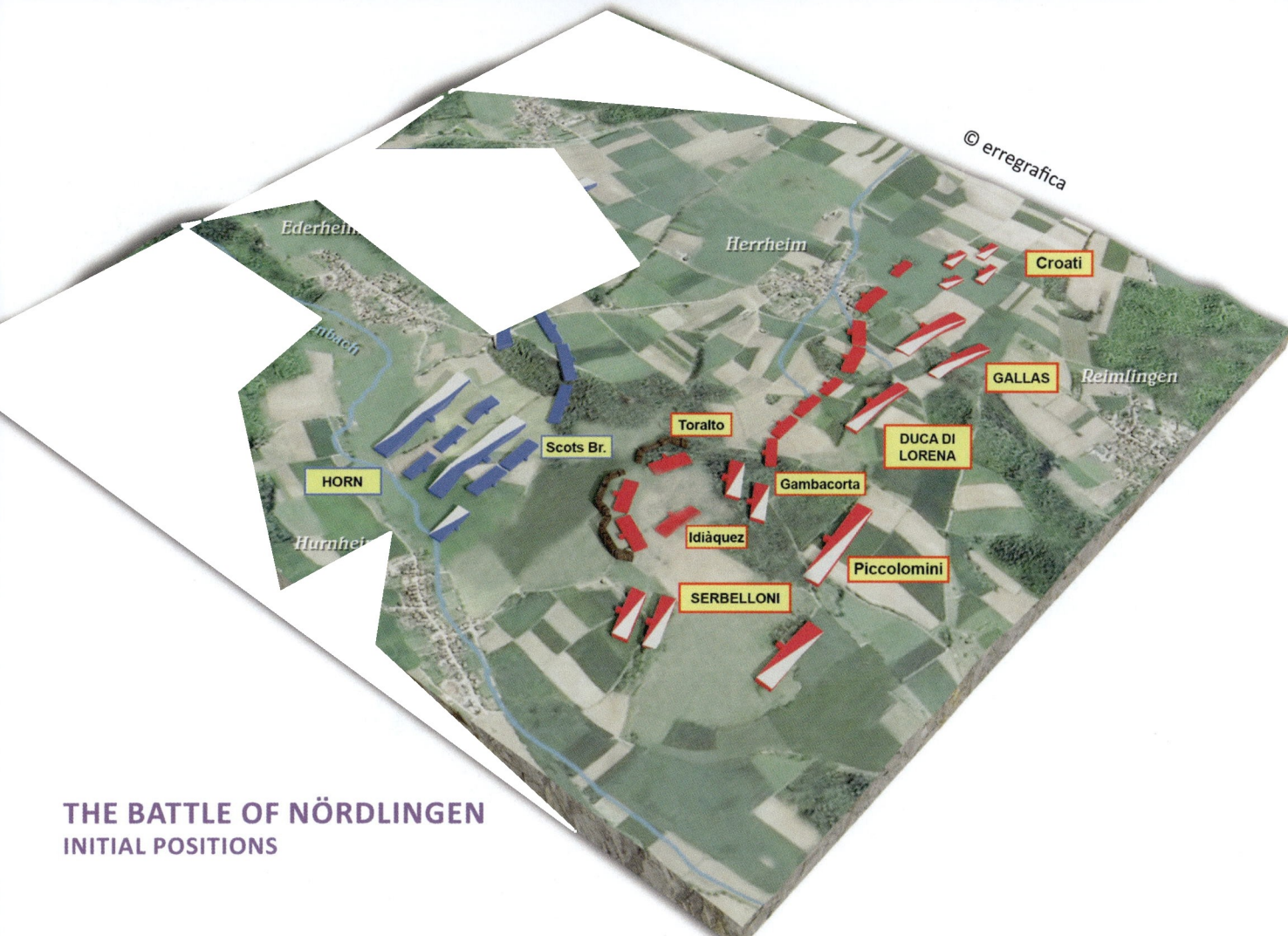

THE BATTLE OF NÖRDLINGEN
INITIAL POSITIONS

cavalrymen and a few hundred dragoons) and finally what survived of the Spanish army of Feria after the typhus epidemic (3,300 infantrymen and 1,080 cavalrymen).

The true strength of the imperial army was actually the unity of command, something the Protestant army could not boast of, as relations between Horn, the Marshal of Sweden, i.e. the commander-in-chief of all Swedish forces and Bernand of Saxony, the commander of the League of Heilbronn, was deteriorating forcing the two to operate autonomously because neither wanted to acknowledge the superiority of the other. Aware of this, Fernando and Gallas aimed to defeat the two armies one by one. The first imperial objective was the fortress of Regensburg. In order to prevent its conquest, Bernard of Saxony's troops tried to block the passage of the rival army that was far more numerous.

Bernard was forced to fall back on Kelheim and ask Horn for help, who, seeing the strategic importance of Regensburg, reluctantly lifted the siege of Uberingen to converge on the Bavarian city. The Protestants joined forces on 12 July in Augsburg. The aim was to put Bavaria to the torch in order to force the Catholics to lift the siege on Regensburg, which had begun a month earlier. Freisung and Moosburg were conquered, while in Landshut they defeated the corps of Aldringen, who died in battle. However, the strategy proved useless because the Imperials do not abandon the siege and Regensburg capitulated a few days later.

The other bad news that reached the ears of the Protestant commanders in those days was that a second Spanish army under the command of Cardinal-Infante Ferdinand was coming from Milan and, was in Tyrol and marching towards Bavaria.

THE BATTLE

At dawn on 3 September, in front of the fortress of Nördlingen, the combined armies of the Cardinal-Infante and his cousin Ferdinand of Hungary lined up for battle. Presenting an ultimatum to the city, the Protestants defending it decided not to surrender, knowing that the Swedish-Saxon army was but two days' march away. On 4 September, the

Catholics began bombarding the defensive positions of Nördlingen and then made an assault, which was repulsed after three hours of hard fighting with around 500 casualties inflicted on the attackers. Meanwhile, Horn and Bernardo disagreed on how to intervene. The Swedish marshal feared the numerical superiority of the Catholics (whom he estimated outnumbered the protestant forces 3 to 2) and advocated waiting for the arrival of about 10,000 reinforcements (3,400 under Cratz's command and 6,000 under Rhinegrave's orders) He was also convinced that the Spanish army was only passing through and that the Cardinal-Infante's objective remained Flanders. Horn therefore proposed taking more time sacrificing the city of Nördlingen but not his army. Bernand nevertheless convinced him of a plan to carry out a flanking manoeuvre aimed at both joining Cratz's men and cutting the imperial supply lines. On 5 June, news that the Protestant army was on the move reached the Catholic camp where a new attack on the city was being prepared. It took the Imperialists and the Spaniards a while to realise that their adversaries were not moving away from the city to leave it to its fate, but carrying out a circumventing manoeuvre. The Catholic army, divided into three commands (the Spaniards on the left, the Catholic League in the centre and the Imperials on the right) thus prepares for the pitched battle, yet there was no sign of the Protestants. In fact, the scouts reported that Bernand and Horn had moved further south to join Cratz's forces.

Having achieved their objective, the Protestant commanders headed north to engage the opposing army. The first clashes, in the late afternoon of 5 June, involved their cavalry units, supported by musketeers and dragoons. They fought mainly for control of the Heselberg forest, which the Spanish had identified as a strategic point. After several attacks, Cratz's cavalry was pushed back, at which point Bernard of Saxony launched three of his best cavalry regiments in a charge. However, the hilly terrain created visibility and deployment problems for his troops forcing Bernard to move men to his right and to widen the front line.

The clashes between Saxon and Spanish cavalry regiments were fierce and involved around 6,000 men, but ultimately proved inconclusive and shortly before sunset both sides were forced to retreat. Meanwhile, the battle continued around the forest and in particular in a contest to control the Heselberg hill. For this objective, however,

Bernard needed reinforcements from Horn, who was unable to reach the battlefield before nightfall and only managing to deploy for battle after midnight. Realising that the forest would be lost, Cardinal-Infante ordered Count Serbelloni to reinforce the position on the Albuch hill, considered to be the next focal point of the battle. At 11 p.m. the Protestants charged the forest once again in force with about 4,000 men and by 11.30 p.m. they succeeded in taking it as the Spanish defenders retreated to the adjacent Albuch Hill in anticipation of the final clash the next day.

Dawn on the 6th of June found the Protestant army exhausted from 20 hours of marching and fighting and the Catholics controlling the Albuch hill overlooking the battlefield. Horn was of the opinion that to continue the battle was suicide and advocated retreat. Bernard of Saxony was of a different opinion, convinced that one more push would be enough to make the Catholic army, which was just as exhausted by the previous day's fighting, to give way. In the end it was once again Bernard who prevailed and at 5 a.m. the Protestant assault on the hill of Albuch began.

The Swedish-German army had 16,300 infantrymen, 9,300 cavalrymen and 62 cannons divided into two wings, one under the command of Horn and the other of Bernard. Their objective was the capture of the Albuch hill, from which they could threaten the Catholic army's lines of supply and retreat. In front of them, Ferdinand of Hungary and his cousin Cardinal-Infante had 23,000 infantrymen, 13,000 cavalrymen and 65 cannons: a considerable numerical advantage, as well as a good defensive position. The Catholic army was divided into three distinct corps: the Spaniards under the command of the Marquis of Leganés, Diego Mexía de Guzmán y Davila (assisted by Count Serbelloni, who also commanded the artillery) on the left flank, south of Nördlingen; the Catholic League troops in the centre (under the orders of Duke Charles IV of Lorraine) and the imperial troops, under the command of Matthias Gallas, on the right (closer to Nördlingen). The defenders of the hill, mostly veterans possessed three redoubts.

The assault on the hill fell to the Swedes, who were reinforced by some 7,000 Saxon and Wurttemberg soldiers. It was up to the Saxon general Johan Vitzhum to first test the formidable Catholic defences. His infantrymen and cavalrymen were met by the fire of the 14 cannons placed on the Albuch and, by fire from musketeers. The Protestant cavalry launched on the assault was effectively counter-charged on the flank by that of the La Tour regiment. Vitzhum's infantry, left without support, aimed at the central redoubt and managed to dislodge the defenders (German Salm and Wurmuster regiments). Piccolomini seeing the Catholic line compromised, ordered Gambacorta's cavalry to attack Vitzhum's men, with the support of the Idiaquez tercio that was in reserve behind the three redoubts. Meanwhile Horn launched his second attack by advancing two new brigades. This time the target was the northernmost redoubt defended by the Neapolitan tercio Toralto.

The hill became the scene of bloody clashes of multiple protestant attacks with the units falling back regrouping and charging again. Around 7.30 a.m., however, it became clear to Horn that the assault had not brought the desired result; the Catholic defences do not give way. He therefore asked Bernard, whose task it had been planned was to attack the rest of the opposing army once the Albuch hill had been taken, to intervene. Up to that point, Bernard had been engaged in a series of minor skirmishes, mainly against the Croatian light cavalry. The Saxon therefore ordered the Thurn brigade, consisting of the Protestant army's two elite (Swedish) regiments, the Black and the Yellow, to support the attack on the hill.

Seeing Thurn's men approaching, Horn ordered his cavalry to prepare to provide the necessary support. The cavalry, however, misinterpreted the Swedish marshal's intentions causing the assault to go in without support. Even so, the Thurn brigade comprised of some 3,500 fresh men were advancing against 1,650 exhausted defenders but the Italians of the Toralto unleashed such fire on the attackers that they pinned them to the ground long before they could reach the parapets. Thurn's men also suffered cross-fire from the artillery and, seeing them exposed, Piccolomini and Gambacorta decided to charge them with cavalry (just over 2,000 men). Sensing imminent disaster, Horn launched his own cavalry, which was repulsed. Left alone again, Thurn's men managed to hold out heroically for an hour and a half until the Spaniards of the tercio Idiaquez decided to leave their defensive position to attack them. The two Swedish regiments, which by that time had sustained 50 per cent casualties, retreated. At that point, about 9.30 a.m., Piccolomini ordered the general advance.

Meanwhile on the Protestant left wing, Bernard, who had just launched a charge of 2,000 of his cuirassiers against the Catholic positions along the Herkheimefeld plateau, was joined by Horn, who, seeing the deteriorating situation on the right wing, wanted to order a retreat. This time the Swedish marshal succeeded, not without difficulty, in convincing the Saxon, who, remained certain that he could still hold on that side, allowing Horn to retreat in good order and stand in the woods around Arnsberg. However, contrary to his expectations, Bernard's cavalry was defeated quickly and the general advance ordered by Gallas sealed the Protestant defeat. What remained of the Swedish-Saxon army was surrounded and finished off with great slaughter by the Croatian and Bavarian cavalry. Horn was also taken prisoner and all the protestant artillery was captured.

The Battle of Nordlingen, which led to the Peace of Prague (30 May 1635) and the dissolution of the League of Heilbronn, also marked the end of Swedish supremacy. The Battle also marked the return to prominence of the Tercio, which had been too hastily dismissed as obsolete. It would be the French, nine years later, who would sanction its end at the famous Battle of Rocroi.

POSSIBLE SCENARIOS

The battle of Nordlingen can be broken up into many scenarios: the clashes of 5 June, the entire battle of 6 June or simply the battle for the possession of Albuch Hill. Dividing the battle into several clashes saves a lot of miniatures (using losses as reinforcements) and having to set up a good slice/part of the battlefield.

The clashes on 5 June can result in two scenarios. The first involves the cavalry and dragoon units on hilly terrain, with visibility restrictions. The second the assault on the forest, also involving infantry. In this case, the advice is to use the units you want with as much freedom as possible, focusing more on tactical issues.

To replay the clash on Albuch Hill use only Horn's and Piccolomini's commands. Horn may place the yellow and black brigades (from Bernard's command) as reserve, while Piccolomini may draw from the Spanish reserve a Tercio and a unit of Cuirassiers. Reserve Units may come into play when a companion Unit becomes exhausted (from the next turn). Reserve Units must be deployed more than 10BU from the enemy and do not count in the initial VDT, only as losses.

ORDERS OF BATTLE WITH BAROQUE

The following are the orders of battle for Baroque. Depending on your availability and the number of players you can also multiply the number of units by 2 or 3. The VBU of the Tercio was lowered from 8 to 7 to simulate the fact that they were undermanned. The same was done with some German brigades.

PROTESTANTS

Average Command Structure - VDT=58

SAXONY-WEIMAR (VDC=31)
Bernard of Saxony (Poor)
3 TR Cuirassiers M=2S, VBU=6, I=3, D=B, VD=3, PB, Cuirass
3 TR Cuirassiers M=2, VBU=6, I=3, D=B, VD=3, PB Pistol
2 RE Mounted Harquebusiers M=2, VBU=5, D=B, VD=2, Pistol/Carbine, PB Pistol
1 P&M Bernard Brigade M=1, VBU=6, I=2, D=B, VD=2, Pike, Musket (SM-2), Salvo
1 P&M Yellow Brigade M=1, VBU=6, I=2, D=B, VD=2, Pike, Musket (SM-2), Salvo, Hardened
1 P&M Black Brigade M=1, VBU=6, I=2, D=B, VD=2, Pike, Musket (SM-2), Salvo, Hardened, Iron Officers
3 Art M=1S, VBU=1, D=B, VD=1, Art B

SWEDEN (VDC=27)
Marshal Gustav Horn (Reliable)
3 TR latta Ryttare and German Mercenaries M=2, VBU=6, I=3, D=B, VD=3, PB Pistol
2 H&M M=2S, VBU=6, I=2, D=B, VD=3, PB, Musket (MM-3), Salvo
1 TR Reiter M=2, VBU=5, I=1, VD=2, PB Pistol

1 DR, Dragoons M=2, VBU=5, I=1, D=B, VD=2, Musket
1 P&M Scots and Pfhul Brigade M=1, VBU=6, I=2, D=A, VD=3, Pike, Musket (SM-2), Salvo, Hardened, Iron Officers, Regimental Artillery
2 P&M Infantry M=1, VBU=6, I=2, D=B, VD=2, Pike, Musket (SM-2), Salvo
1 Art M=1S, VBU=1, D=B, VD=1, Art B

CATHOLICS
Good Command Structure - VDT=66

SPANISH (VDC=25)
Piccolomini (Expert)
3 TR Cuirassiersi M=2, VBU=6, I=3, D=B, VD=3, PB Pistol
1 ETE Tercio Toralto M=1S, VBU=7, I=2, D=B, VD=4, Pike, Musket, (SM-4), MM4, Feared, Hardened
1 ETE Tercio Idiaquez M=1S, VBU=7, I=2, D=B, VD=4, Pike, Musket, (SM-4), MM4, Feared, Hardened
1 DR, Dragoons M=2, VBU=5, I=1, D=B, VD=2, Musket
1 P&M Salm&Wurmuster Brigade M=1, VBU=5, I=2, D=B, VD=2, Pike, Musket (SM-2)
1 P&M Leslie&Fugger Brigade M=1, VBU=5, I=2, D=B, VD=2, Pike, Musket (SM-2)
2 P&M Other German brigades M=1, VBU=5, I=2, D=B, VD=2, Pike, Musket (SM-2)
1 T Italian detached musketeers M=1, VBU=4, I=0, D=B, VD=2, Musket
2 Art M=1S, VBU=1, D=B, VD=1, Art B
3 Fortifications

CATHOLIC LEAGUE (VDC=16)
Duke of Lorraine (Poor)
2 TR Bavarian Cuirassiers M=2, VBU=6, I=3, D=B, VD=3, PB Pistol
3 P&M Germans M=1, VBU=5, I=2, D=B, VD=2, Pike, Musket (SM-2)
1 DR, Dragoons M=2, VBU=5, I=1, D=B, VD=2, Musket
2 Art M=1S, VBU=1, D=B, VD=1, Art B

IMPERIAL (VDC=25)
Gallas (Expert)
2 TR Armourers M=2, VBU=6, I=3, D=B, VD=3, PB Pistol
2 CL Croatians M=2F, VBU=4, I=1, D=B, VD=2, Pistol/carbine
1 DR, Dragoons M=2, VBU=5, I=1, D=B, VD=2, Musket
1 P&M, Guardsmen M=1, VBU=6, I=2, D=A, VD=3, Pike, Musket (SM-2), Hardened, Iron officers
4 German P&M M=1, VBU=5, I=2, D=B, VD=2, Pike, Musket (SM-2)
2 Art M=1S, VBU=1, D=B, VD=1, Art B

RESERVE
(For balancing reasons does not count for VDT, but only as losses)
2 TR Cuirassiers M=2, VBU=6, I=3, D=B, VD=3, PB
2 P&M Germans M=1, VBU=5, I=2, D=B, VD=2, Pike, Musket (SM-2)
1 ETE Tercio M=1S, VBU=7, I=2, D=B, VD=4, Pike, Musket, (SM-4), MM4, Hardened

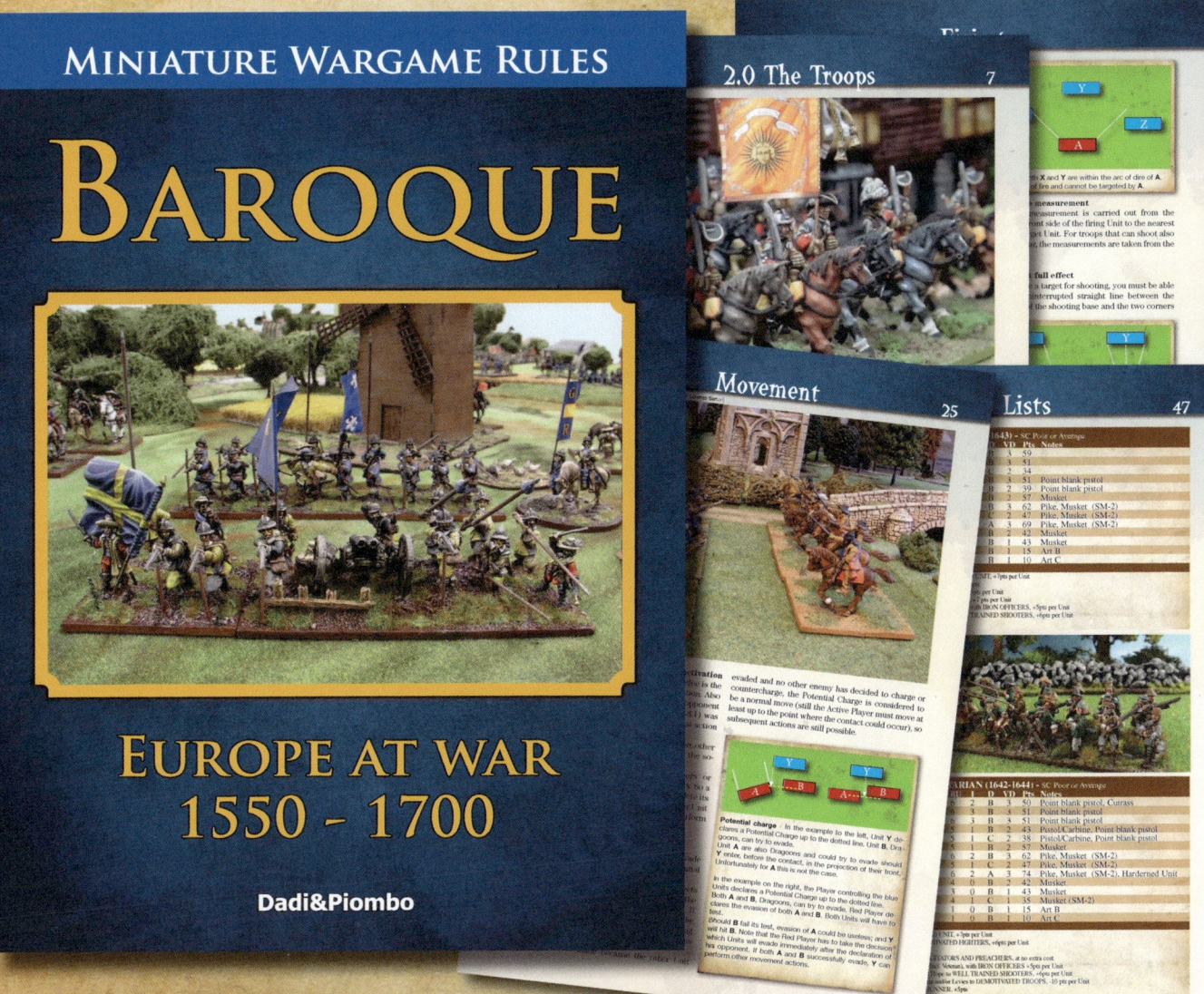

❖ Baroque is a set of wargames rules, based on the Impetus system. The rules allow you to play using miniatures the wars that ravaged Europe from the mid XVI Cent to the end of the XVII Cent.

❖ Baroque is easy to learn and combines fast, enjoyable play with historical accuracy thanks to the innovative game-mechanics.

❖ Baroque can be played in all scales: 28mm, 20mm, 15mm, 10mm and 6mm, and you won't even need to re-base your armies.

❖ Baroque rulebook includes the rules (with many examples and diagrams) to fight the battles. It includes seven army lists which will allow you to start playing right away: German Catholics (1618-32), Swedish (1630-34), ECW Royalist (1642-43), ECW Parliamentarian (1642-44), Ottoman Turks (1645-1700), Later Imperialist (1648-1700), Later Polish (1632-1700). Many more lists can be downloaded for free from www.dadiepiombo.com

BUY YOUR COPY NOW
On Amazon (Amazon edition)
Through our shop (spiral bound edition)
As PDF through wargamevault.com

www.dadiepiombo.com

PAINTING WITH CONTRAST

by STEFANO IZZO

INTRODUCTION

In our placid and sleepy milieu of 'toy soldier painting', few new things are currently happening, although in the past, some trends have undoubtedly had an 'epochal' impact. For example, the switch from enamels to acrylics in the name of practicality and health, the use of 'inks' to simulate shading, and the use of washes with special shadow tints to accentuate chiaroscuro, but little else has occurred.

But recently, there has been increasing talk in our obscure circles of a technique that would have something 'miraculous' about it: 'transparency' painting, also commonly known as the "contrast technique" is named after the first line of colours specifically developed for this type of painting.

What is it? In a few words, the figure is first prepared with a very light base of white, pale grey or ivory before the actual colours are applied using a single coat of special paints that have the characteristic of covering at the right point but maintaining a good deal of transparency while thickening in the recesses and maintaining the light base in the reliefs.

By exploiting the light background of the toy soldier and the transparency of the colours, with a single brush stroke of a single colour, a 'shading' effect is obtained by flooding the hollows and convexities of the model sculpture. It does not require too much time when compared to the much longer and more pains taking chiaroscuro work obtained with traditional techniques of successive coats of lighter or darker colours.

This painting technique and the resulting range of colours was developed by Games Workshop with the primary objective of reducing the time and difficulty in painting miniatures, a fundamental aspect for a company that has always produced paints, but above all games and miniatures themselves.

The time required to paint a number of models has always been a major obstacle to the growth of the hobby, and this is why GW has gone to great lengths to invent painting techniques that allow us gamers to spend less time painting our armies and the company to successfully market more complex and numerous miniatures.

In this sense, the 'Contrast' range represents an major development in GW's tried-and-tested 'Ink' range, which was already used to create a chiaroscuro effect. The difference lies in the fact that with the 'Ink' technique a figure is first painted in the basic colours then darkened through 'inks', whereas in the 'Contrast' technique a figure is base painted only using one of the abovementioned base colours that are then painted and 'shaded' with a single coat of semi-transparent paint. Indeed, as far as I have seen, no technique allows painting times to be reduced as much as the by the transparency technique, while still maintaining satisfactory results.

In view of these undoubted advantages, many manufacturers have now put their own 'semi-transparent' paint lines on the market. In addition to GW with its 'Contrast' line, we also have Army Painter with its 'Speed Paint' line, Warcolours with its 'Antithesis' line, Scale 75 with its 'Instant colours', and I hope I have not forgotten too many others.

But was all this a real "breakthrough" by the companies that brought these new paints to market? Yes and no. No, because many veteran painters knew this technique and had been practicing it for some time. I myself painted some armies many years ago starting with a white base and coating over the figure with Vallejo acrylic paints diluted with "Matt varnish" and a little water. The effect, I can assure you, is very similar to that of today's "contrast" paints. But one could answer yes, because undoubtedly having ready-to-use paints is a great convenience and because in any case the continued experimental work of the large companies will further perfect this technique making it more and more usable.

ADVANTAGES AND DISADVANTAGES

Of the advantages already mentioned, and they are indeed undeniable, the speed of execution is the first of them since each colour requires only one coat, without the need to waste further time in creating the chiaroscuro. The painting time of each piece is reduced to much less than half with appreciable results, I can guarantee this. Another advantage is the possibility that in using these paints even the less expe-

rienced painter will achieve satisfactory results without too much difficulty. But beware, all that glitters is not gold, as the technique of transparency is not fool proof and still must be practiced. It has its pitfalls.

A first problem is suggested by the very name of the technique "by transparency." It requires that you paint over a light base coat so, if you "smudge" a co-

lour, you will be forced, almost always, to restore the light background before applying again. Additionally, by passing a second semi-transparent colour on top of another semi-transparent colour, the results could be rather unpleasant. Therefore, it is a technique that requires a precision perhaps slightly easier than the traditional technique, but if you err here and there and don't

correct by restoring the light ground before applying the next coat don't expect miracles.

A second limitation is presented by the difficulties of semi-transparent colours remain fixed on very large and convex surfaces. In these circumstances, a colour that is not controlled can produce an ugly "blotchy" effect. Attention must be paid, in particular, to those more or less extensive areas in which the colour tends to settle too much, creating dark clots that can be absorbed with the brush when the colour is still wet, but are completely irretrievable when the colour is dry.

In addition, when using these paints, you will notice that their darkening in the areas where the colour settles is exponential and not progressive, in the sense that large clusters of colour or, worse still, drops quickly tend to take on much darker tones than the relative transparency of a thin layer (e.g. certain yellows, settling and drying in the recesses, becoming a sort of dark brown, etc.).

Also, remember that, by using these lightly covering colours, it is practically impossible to remedy errors and, in most cases, it will be necessary to start again from the light background and redo from scratch that colour which has come out wrong, so watch out.

A third pitfall lies in the fact that semi-transparent colours, as opposed to opaque colours, are sensitive to 'second coats': if you apply paint twice on one part of the model and once on others, the difference in shade will be noticeable.

Another issue concerns the characteristics of the single colours. So far, I have only tried GW's 'Contrast' colours and have noticed very strong differences in the rendering between one colour and another, in the sense that some are more transparent, others less so, which is not good. To get around this problem, it is necessary to know the qualities of each colour through tests and possibly increase the transparency of some through the appropriate thinner.

A fifth limitation that the more finicky painter will notice is that you must apply the same base colour to all the figures. That is to say, the light "primer" (white, grey or ivory) with which you prepare the like pieces must be the same. This ensures that all the "transparencies" will be of the same tone, regardless of whether they are lighter areas of a warm colour or a cold colour. Regarding the range of use of this technique, these paints do their best work on highly detailed surfaces, not too lar-

ge but not too small either; they were developed, in short, for 28 mm figures. I believe that for the lower scales other painting processes with greater chiaroscuro are more suitable for emphasising minute details (e.g. the black background), while for larger scales the presence of extensive surfaces could lead, with the use of these paints, to the proliferation of shadows or spots that I have already mentioned that are unpleasant to the eye.

In conclusion to this brief examination of "pros and cons" it must be added that in the range of semi-transparent colours there are, for reasons that are easy to understand, no metallic shades, for which you will therefore have to resort to your traditional colours.

HINTS ON TECHNIQUE

As I said earlier, if at first glance the 'transparency' technique seems simple and intuitive, it is in fact not so easy to master and, considering that I have been using it habitually for about a couple of years now, I would like to pass on some of my experiences.

First of all, the "primer" plays a decisive role. These paints are made to run on smooth surfaces and thicken in the recesses so the priming process is absolutely fundamental for a good end result. Therefore, choose a "primer" that leaves the surfaces as smooth as possible; otherwise, with a porous and dusty primer, painting "by transparency" will give very poor results as the semi-transparent colour will not flow over the surfaces remaining thick, negating all the good properties of these paints and all your legitimate aspirations.

Regarding the colour of the "primer", it must be very light and very bright, varying between a very pale grey and ivory, depending on whether you want a cooler or warmer end result. Whatever base colour you choose, keep some of it at hand, because when you "smudge" with some semi-transparent colour, it will serve to restore the light background before applying the next colour.

In application, the semi-transparent colours should be applied without being "pulled" across the surface. They should be allowed to almost drop from the brush to the surface in moderate quantities, so that they are free to flow briefly and settle on the surfaces on their own, but without going so far as to form real "drops" of colour which, as they dry, would give rise to the undesirable stains we have talked about.

I recommend that you use brushes that are small but not too small with a tip that is not too long, so that you have a fairly capable "reservoir" of paint but is still controllable. If drips form, you must disperse them or pick them up with the brush tip quickly, well before they begin to dry. Be careful and keep a close eye on the performance of the coat, because transparent colours tend to dry very quickly.

In particular, keep a close eye on both the deeper recesses, where 'channels' of colour may thicken, and the broader reliefs, where the colour should remain light and transparent to highlight areas. These darker, colour thickenings in the midst of light are the worst that can happen.

As I mentioned earlier, not all semi-transparent colours have the same yield: some are very light and can be applied as they are, others tend to co-

ver too much and it may be necessary, depending on your taste, to make them more transparent through the use of special thinners or, sometimes even water is sufficient, depending on the composition of the paints produced by the various companies.

In any case, when using a colour for the first time it is best to try it first on other light surfaces to check that the transparency effect is consistent with the result you want to achieve.

Ideally, try to divide the model into areas well delimited by raised details (e.g. the bust from the shoulders to the waist) and cover each individual area with a single coat of paint before it dries, as a second coat of semi-transparent paint on an already dry area changes the final result compared to areas that have only received one pass.

I repeat, after the glazes have dried it is very difficult to change a bad end result, so care must be taken and an attempt must be made to fix everything that can be corrected while the colour is still wet, otherwise the area will have to be covered again with primer and the whole process of applying the colour that went wrong will have to be repeated.

SOME SECRETS OF THE TRADE

I have already given some tips for achieving better results such as getting to know, and possibly diluting, the various colours, avoiding "double coats", checking drips and stains, etc. Now, I would like to add something for the benefit of those of you who, even if using "semi-transparencies", do not feel completely satisfied because of a final result that is too evanescent and poorly defined, seeming not very "linear" compared to traditional gradient painting. The risk is there, because figures painted all in semi-transparent colours on a uniform light background can end up looking sometimes too ... "transparent". So, what can be done? How can we achieve more muted chiaroscuro even with little pigment and a common base tone for all colours? In most cases, I tend to blend various techniques to achieve greater contrasts, in particular the one in question with the more traditional ones of "washes" (total or partial) and, more rarely, also with the "dry brush". Firstly, even though semi-transparent colours already guarantee a chiaroscuro effect, before applying them I do not refrain from giving the white background a quick wash of shadow-coloured 'ink', taking care that it does not thicken too much and sparing as much as possible the details which must remain white or which are very much in the light (e.g. the highest part of the shoulder).

It is inadvisable to use this technique on white garments and on fabrics that must give a very "vaporous" effect (such as cloaks, etc.), but the results in all other cases are effective, because the semi-transparent colours passed over the shadow ink tend to slightly dampen the excessive contrasts but benefit enormously from the background light and shade. The same technique can, of course, also be used afterward by 'washing' with shadow ink, without overdoing it, certain areas that have already been coloured with the semi-transparent colours but which, in your opinion, require more contrast or detail.

I don't want to advertise one company to the detriment of others, but to do this delicate work of "total shading", or even selective shading, I have so far experienced the best results with GW's Agrax Earthshade (as is) or Vallejo's Black Glaze and Brown Glaze mixed together and diluted with a little water to obtain the shadow tone.

So far, we have talked about how to accentuate the shadow areas with semi-transparent colours to emphasise the highlights. But it is also difficult once the paints are dry, to obtain a tone that is compatible with the lighter areas obtained by "transparency." This can often be achieved by mixing a certain amount of the semi-transparent colour that you have used with a colour similar or equal to the light background of the model, but you have to try it out each time and the result is not always guaranteed.

In fact, if you want to lighten a certain colour which, although semi-transparent, still seems too dark or too opaque, it is better to act 'upstream'. That is, before painting, by preparing a more diluted version of the same colour to be kept in special bottles, so that it can be used in other circumstances.

This is the technique I personally use to paint the fabrics of my 'ancients.' It should not be forgotten, in fact, that many semi-transparent colour lines have been developed with an eye to the fantasy genre, so the colours are often very bright. Therefore, I tend to obtain more 'washed-out' and luminous tones of the same colours with the addition of thinner.

In this regard, I would like to point out that, once the paint is dry, it is possible to pass a second coat over a colour that has become too transparent, but it is not possible to lighten a tone that is too dark or too bright, so in this case 'melius deficere quam abundare' that

is, better too little than too much and meditate before covering too much.

As you are painting and, while the paint is still wet, you can also work on individual areas that you want to lighten by placing a little thinner on the tip of the brush, in order to remove pigment and give more transparency to the highlights. So, when painting it is always a good idea to have some thinner on hand to correct highlights and a small bottle of the basic white, grey, or ivory tone available to correct any mistakes.

In conclusion, I think that the 'transparency' technique is a great step forward in our hobby, and not only because it speeds up enormously the painting of our little monsters. That it is a way of painting that, once mastered, has advantages over traditional techniques. It can also be used with advantage in the painting of larger and more "noble" subjects than the simple wargame figure, at least for certain details or to create specific effects.

It is a painting technique that is perhaps relatively easy to implement at a basic stage, but no less difficult to master at a higher level than other traditional techniques. The secret is to know each individual colour and to modify the degree of dilution if necessary to proceed and, to obtain the best results, by the application of light and successive transparencies, so as to be able to gradually meld light and shadow.

It is a technique of painting that, understandably, is rapidly gaining popularity due to its speed, so one can also expect a progressive refinement in the quality of both the paints and the colours dedicated to it. This may take time so let us not forget how much time and how many developments were necessary to reach the current technical level of traditional paints, whether oils, enamels or acrylics.

In short, I recommend you try it, also because I find, most importantly, that painting 'by transparency' is a particularly dynamic and fun way of painting, as you can see the results of each pass of colour "live" with a practically immediate effect, shading included!

All photos refer to 28mm scale Victrix brand soldiers, painted by the author using the "by transparency" technique and belonging to his collection.

HUSSITES
THE FAITH, THE CHALICE AND THE WAGON

by RENATO GENOVESE

On 6 July 1415, the religious reformer Jan Hus was burnt at the stake in Constance, southern Germany. Hungary's King Sigismund of Luxembourg had requested a church Council in that city, and Hus—a Bohemian preacher and early Protestant—had travelled there in good faith.

Huss was prepared to argue his religious theses before the assembly of cardinals, but after a stormy first hearing, he was instead arrested and put on trial (see the box below "The Holy Chalice"). In reality, he had been lured into a trap, even though the sovereign had promised him safe-conduct to defend himself against the charge of heresy. The Council's sentence was inevitable: death. The Church was so fearful of the risk of a schism that the execution of Hus was particularly thorough, as if to completely erase all traces of his physical presence on earth: [...] then the executioners pulled down the toasted limbs [...] they burnt them further, bringing more wood to the fire [...] Then, walking round and round, they broke the bones with clubs to make them burn faster. When they found the head, they broke it to pieces with clubs and threw it on the fire. When they found the heart in the midst of the entrails, after they had sharpened a stick like a spit, they pierced it at the tip and took special care to roast and consume it, poking it with their spears, until it was reduced to ashes [...] they loaded all the ashes onto a cart and threw it into the Rhine [...].

But the thoroughness and brutality of his death did not eradicate Jan Hus' influence. On the contrary, by making him a martyr, the Church and the Empire had created for themselves a terrible thorn in their side which, for some twenty years, turned a large portion of the Czech people into a stubborn and unexpectedly unbeatable enemy: the Hussites.

THE END OF THE MIDDLE AGES

The end of the Middle Ages was marked by a loss of economic security, combined with the intrigues of politics and brutal military campaigns. Europe had entered the 15th century amid an upheaval, and many of its hitherto shared values were called into question. The unity of the Church had been shaken by a great schism in which two popes, one Roman and the other Avignonese fought not only for spiritual dominance but also for the favour of the various sovereigns. The rivalry cast an increasingly dark shadow over spiritual and ecclesiastical life. For four decades there was no force capable of negotiating a truce, let alone peace.

Additionally, a moral decadence had infected Bohemia and its Church. The Pisan antipope Baldasarre Cossa (called John XXIII), hungry for money, had launched a campaign to sell indulgences—a practice which outraged many devout Christians, especially the reformist Hus and his followers. The high ranking clergy in the archiepiscopal seat in Prague devoted itself wholeheartedly to the lucrative new business, while the poorly educated country clergy allowed themselves to be dragged into the malpractice, showing themselves unfit to guide the souls of the faithful. The protocol of the Archdeaconry Inspection of 1379-1382 exposed the terrible conditions of the country clergy, finding them endowed with little conscience and little education. It specifically cited drunkenness, gambling, the fathering of children as well as the general lack of knowledge of liturgical literature.

Adding to this deep spiritual crisis were continuous petty feudal wars between local noble families. Some lords maintained large armed groups, veritable gangs of malefactors, that robbed travellers, attacked neighbouring properties and terrorized peasants. The people of the countryside, although they were the main producers of wealth for the country, were the most exposed and defenceless against all attacks. Additionally, being at the bottom of the economic and social ladder, they faced increasingly heavy taxes. When, at the turn of the 14th and 15th century, the Central Court decided that the peasants could no longer lodge complaints against their lords, the situation of the rural populations worsened quickly. The exasperated peasants, especially in Southern Bohemia, gladly heeded revo-

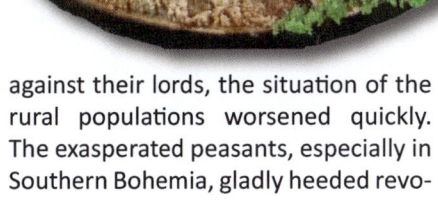

lutionary appeals first made by Hus, in the belief that a future world of justice and spirituality could only be achieved through their own active intervention.

FROM THE STAKE TO THE SWORD

Popular outrage over Hus's death in 1415 led to the foundation of and insurrectionist movement inspired by his views. The movement split into the moderate Calixtines or Utraquists, and the radical Taborites. The name of "Taborite" had a rather singular origin. On 22 July 1419, they had gathered on a mountain ridge some seventy kilometres south-west of Prague. The Bohemians associated this hill with Mount Tabor the one mentioned in the Gospels as the place from which Jesus had undergone the transfiguration. There, energised by the fear of a coming Apocalypse and the certainty of Jesus' imminent return to earth and, supported by the fiery sermons of the radical priests, the connection was taken at face value and the first Hussite fortress-town, Tabor, was founded on the hill. Over time, two even more intransigent movements sprang from the Taborite factions, namely the Horebites and the Adamites.

The Bohemian ruler Wenceslas, initially sympathetic to the Hussites, eventually switched his support to the Church and attempted to exclude the Hussites from public and religious offices. This, in turn, provoked an uprising, and the Taborites immediately militarised under the leadership of a charismatic commander from the lower nobility: Jan Žižka of Trocnov, a valiant and well-known soldier who had participated in the Tannenberg (Grunwald) campaign of 1410 alongside the Poles against the Teutonic Knights. On 30 July 1419, some Taborites, led by Žižka, staged the first Defenestration of Prague. They seized seven magistrates who had refused to release previously imprisoned Taborites and threw them from the windows of the town hall on to the pikes wielded by a crowd below.

BATTLE IN PRAGUE

Žižka's immediate attentions had focused on Prague, where his opponents were rapidly strengthening their own position. Cenek of Wartenburg, now the Queen Dowager's chief advisor--King Wenceslas had died of a stroke on hearing the news of the defenestration of his representatives--had increased the garrison of Prague's royal castle on Hradčany Hill. German mercenaries strengthened this position around the castle on the city's left bank of the Vltava River. Cenek gave strict orders to prevent a planned march on Prague by the Taborites. Žižka, however, moved quickly to occupy the only remaining fortress in the city that had not yet passed into anti-Hussite hands. This was the citadel of Vyšehrad. The garrison there consisted largely of Žižka's old comrades who, having recognised their old one-eyed captain, opened the gates and gave him the fortress. With the arrival of the Taborites, a fierce battle began for control of Prague. A large part of the city's left bank was destroyed, reducing it to a no man's land between the opposing fortresses. Such was the devastation within the city that a citizen's peace conference was called, in which Hussite freedom of worship was guaranteed in exchange for the departure of the Taborites and the surrender of the Vyšehrad fortress. On hearing this, Žižka flew into a rage as he believed that their cause had been betrayed by the weak citizens of Prague, who evidently did not share the Taborites' religious fervour. However, with his men, he left the capital in November 1419, moving to the city of Pilsen.

Emboldened by their easy success in Prague, the royalists led by Sigismund of Luxemburg, the brother of the late King Wenceslas, turned to the bloody

persecution of Hussite settlements. In Kutna Hora, when they grew tired of hangings, citizens and soldiers of the king threw the Hussites down the shafts of the silver mines for which the town was famous. Pilsen was also threatened by the Royalists, and in March 1420, Žižka was forced to send several detachments of the garrison to defend the small Hussite settlements. He soon decided it was best to abandon Pilsen, and moved south toward the Tabor fortress with his remaining force of 400 men, 12 wagons and a handful of horsemen. This march was to become a significant event because the royal army had no intention of giving the Taborites easy passage to their mystical fortress. But the Royalists never imagined that the Hussites carried with them a form of mobile fortress.

THE WAGENBURG

The wagon was the main means of defence that the rebels used to confront the armies which almost always outnumbered their own. The idea was not a new one, as wagon circles (wagenburgs) had long been formed on Europe's eastern plains, particularly against the Ottomans and other cavalry armies. The difference was that the Hussite wagons were not mere barricades, but self-propelled fortresses well equipped with artillery and other firearms, providing unprecedented firepower for the times. In order to cancel out their numerical inferiority, Jan Žižka and his successors resorted heavily to the use of these weapons, which were fairly easy to manufacture owing to the numerous foundries that Prague and other cities were equipped with.

The wagon crews were supplemented by crossbowmen and troops armed

THE HOLY CHALICE

The manifesto of the Hussite creed was contained in the so-called Four ArtiThe manifesto of the Hussite creed was contained in the so-called Four Articles of Prague. Three of these were:
- Freedom for priests to preach the Holy Scriptures in the local language.
- Expropriation of church property and poverty of the clergy.
- Temporal penalties for mortal sins committed by members of the clergy.

But one of the first ways the Hussites expressed their dissent after Hus's death was through a simple but revolutionary religious ritual. Canon Law required the congregation to receive Communion at Mass through consecrated bread (the body of Christ), while the clergy also received wine (his blood). One of the elements of the reform practised in Bohemia by the priests who were followers of Jan Hus (contained in the 2nd Article) was the sharing with the faithful also of the chalice containing the wine, referred to as "Eucharistic Communion in both forms," given to both adults and children. Since the Council of Constance had firmly condemned this practice, the ritual became the mainstay of the movement. Priests who refused to give Communion under both forms were driven out of their churches and replaced with adherents of the reform, who took the name Utraquists, from the Latin expression sub utraqua parte.

Thus, the chalice became the emblem of the Reformed Church of Bohemia and was the symbol contained in the flags of the revolutionary armies, along with the goose, which was a symbolic translation of the name 'Hus' ('husa' in Czech means goose).

with scourges, scythes and pole-arms of various types, including hooks to unhorse horsemen and morning stars with formidable sharp points. The wagons were placed side by side or slightly staggered in depth, while the intervals between them were manned by infantrymen protected by large pavises decorated with religious symbols. These troops were ready to counter-attack, and supported by cavalry. The heavily armoured cavalry was provided by nobles who joined the Hussite cause, while the rest was made up of light cavalry with crossbows and lances", essential for scouting and pursuing the enemy. In battle, the Hussites did not merely hold a field once they had repulsed the enemy, but pursued them, turning defeat into a rout. This was possible because the Hussite army was organised in an exemplary manner compared to other late medieval armies, especially the five Crusader armies sent against them in which armoured and arrogant horsemen were the primary weapon.

In promoting these new and fierce tactics, Žižka's moral directives regarding his men's discipline were clear: "Soldiers of God should generally avoid any wrongdoing; in battle they should not allow themselves to be overcome by fear, but rather hold their positions in order, and they should be wary of claiming enemy booty before the fighting is over. As soon as the fighting is over and the booty has been taken, it should, however, be made available to the common group and no one should keep anything for himself out of greed". And again: "Among us, we do not want to tolerate those who are disloyal and disobedient, liars, thieves, dice-players, plunderers, drunkards and slanderers, lepers and adulterers, as well as lascivious women and all apparent sinners". However, it was the disciplined collaboration of wagons, cannons, infantry and cavalry, whose deployment followed a clear plan, that allowed the Hussites to set up a veritable combined arms operation to defeat their adversaries.

FEW AGAINST MANY

Pope Martin V called for the first crusade against the Hussites, directing all supporters of the Church to gather in Bohemia. Because of this, on his march to Tabor Žižka found himself pursued by an enemy army of several thousand men. In order not to be caught in mid-movement, he stopped at the locality of Sudoměř. Despite being blind in one eye, the Bohemian general could see well and, above all, he could think even better! He immediately realised that this location was perfect for facing the enemy. The clearing where he deployed his wagons had its flanks protected by ponds and marshes. One thousand Knights Hospitallers of Strakonice attacked the war wagons with enormous losses, including Jindřich of Hradec, their commander. After that, another thousand Royalist knights, led by Peter von Konopischt of Sternberg, attempted to outflank their opponents, but were hindered in the swampy terrain. Forced to dismount from their horses, they attempted to advance again, but soon found themselves again bogged down and once more easy prey for the Hussite infantry advancing out of the shelter of the vozová hradba (wagon fortress), who finished them off with maces and flails. The onset of night put an end to the battle and Žižka took the opportunity to disengage from the battered enemy. The battle, although modest in size, revealed the great Hussite captain's superior knowledge of tactics and terrain. It could be described as a true miracle of its time, as a handful of men, including many peasants, women and children, had been able to inflict heavy losses on armoured knights, escaping for home almost unscathed. This victory consolidated the position of Jan Žižka as the undisputed leader of the Hussite armies. He had demonstrated that his tactics were fluid and that he knew how to adapt to the different conditions in which he was called upon to fight.

THE FIRST CRUSADE

By 1420 Sigismund of Luxembourg, who was eager to be appointed King of Bohemia, had gathered yet another crusader army (chroniclers of the time spoke of 100,000 men, but 50,000 should be closer to the correct figure) and entered the country, heading towards Prague. Žižka received urgent calls for help from the city and moved with an army of about 9,000 men northwards. Taking advantage of the fact that the main fortresses (Vyšehrad and Hradčany) remained in the hands of the Royalists, the crusaders invaded the capital, occupying all strategic points—except for one, Vitkov Hill. The conquest of this position would cut off the city from supplies and relief and Žižka immediately occupied it and set his men to building field fortifications and palisades to counter the certain crusader assault.

The crusaders, mostly German and Hungarian horsemen, attacked but broke against the Hussite field works – even though they were allegedly garrisoned by only 26 men and 3 women. Žižka arrived and realised that the hesitant enemy troops were unsure of what to do, so he unleashed his own furious assault on their flank, routing them and chasing them down the hill. In "The Hussite Wars - Vol. 2", Alexander Querengässer quotes the chronicler Laurentius: "And when the enemies had seen the Sacrament and heard the tolling of the little bell and the loud cries of the people, they turned away overwhelmed with increasing fear, for they hastened to flee from there... Because they ran with such haste, they could not stop and many fell from the top of the cliff and broke their necks, while many were killed by the pursuers". Since then, the hill's name is called Zitkov in honour of Jan Žižka, and one of his most powerful equestrian depictions stands on its summit.

It was clear that the Crusaders would never be able to hold Prague, not least because keeping tens of thousands of men in the field was financially unsu-

PIPPO SPANO

Pippo Spano portrayed by Andrea del Castagno

This is the name by which this foe of the Hussites—a Florentine merchant, and later nobleman and condottiere--went down in history. Born into a noble family in 1369 (his real name was Filippo Buondelmonti degli Scolari), he left for Hungary at the age of 14 following a merchant from his city. In time, thanks to his manners, his elegance and a lucky marriage, he made his way into the Hungarian administration where he acquired his nickname due to the translation of the Hungarian title of governor, ispàn, as 'spano'. Eventually he rose to the court of Sigismund of Luxembourg, soon becoming one of its leading commanders. In this capacity he led victorious campaigns against the Ottomans, supressed numerous uprisings in Bosnia and successfully fought against the Venetian Republic between 1411 and 1413. He proved himself to be particularly ferocious against the vanquished whose right hands he had cut off, in accordance with a custom he had surely brought with him from the campaigns in Hungary and the Balkans. In the campaigns of 1420 and 1422 against Jan Žižka's Hussites, he was one of King Sigismund of Luxembourg's main generals. At Vitkov in particular, he tried to deceive his enemies by feigning an attack on Prague and then turning all his forces against the hill where the Hussites were entrenched. The rebel troops placed in defence of the capital at first remained in place waiting for an attack that did not come. When they finally realised Spano's ruse, they sprang to the attack just as Žižka's fighters were about to succumb to the overwhelming numbers of their adversaries. Despite the resulting disastrous defeat suffered by the crusader army, the Italian remained in the good graces of Emperor Sigismund, who attended his funeral in homage when he died in 1426.

stainable for the king of Hungary. Sigismund thus announced that he was ready to negotiate as long as the Hussites acknowledged him as King of Bohemia. His proposal was accepted and on 28 July 1420 he was crowned in St Vitus Cathedral. But things did not go well for the new king. His troops, already weary from battle, were hit by various epidemics and hated by all the people of Prague, both Hussites and Latin-rite Christians (it is not yet appropriate to call them Catholics). Most of the Germans went home, and Sigismund retreated to Kutna Hora with his remaining soldiers--ending the First Crusade against the Hussites.

INDOMITABLE AND UNBEATABLE

Four more crusades were proclaimed between 1421 to 1431, but their results were also disappointing. Even after Žižka's death in October of 1421, the Hussite armies proved unbeatable. The Hussites were even able, from 1427 to 1431, to launch their own raids outside Bohemian territory. These raids, called "beautiful rides", were intended to relieve pressure from the neighbouring states and to retaliate for the devastation suffered in the Hussite territories, under the offensive strategy advocated by the new leader Andreas Prokop "Veliky" called "The Great." The targets of these raids--Silesia, Austria, Bavaria, Saxony and Brandenburg--formed a league against the Hussites, but it too was defeated at the battles of Mies (1427) and Taus (1431).

In addition, the Hussites allied with the Polish king Ladislaus II Jagellon, who allowed passage of a Hussite army to invade the territories of the Teutonic Knights. The Knights were supported by Pope Eugene IV and the emperor, as well as the Hussites' long-standing enemy, Sigismund of Luxembourg, king of Hungary and Bohemia.

The Hussite army, led by Jan Capek ze San, ravaged the Teutonic territories for more than four months, conquering several towns and several castles. However, they ran into difficulties when the settlements were too heavily fortified, as in the case of the town of Konitz where, after six weeks of fruitless siege, they were forced to retreat. Nevertheless, they pushed north of Danzig and filled their wineskins with water from the Baltic. But by this time, the Hussites were fighting for booty like any other medieval army. This was contrary to what Jan Žižka had preached and, perhaps, led to a weakening of the reform movement.

The Catholics, unable to defeat the Hussites in the field, finally offered negotiation and concessions: at the Council of Basel (1431-1439) they came to the drafting of the Compactata, a series of doctrinal dispensations, which acknowledged the Four Articles of Prague. The implementation, however, was left to the interpretation of Sigismund and the pope -- a compromise the Taborite faction refused to tolerate. This led to a fratricidal war waged between the Utraquists sect (temporarily allied with the Latin-rite Christians) and the Taborites, which ended with the latter's defeat at the Battle of Lipau (or Lipany) on 30 May 1434, where Prokop was killed putting an end to the Hussite wars.

Despite the Compactata agreement--which, among other things, provided for the conferral of numerous offices to Czech nobles, who took advantage of this to regain lost power and privileges--most religious and political issues remained unresolved. Bohemia emerged from the Hussite Wars shattered and impoverished, more feudalized, and with a peasant class practically reduced to servitude. However, Jan Hus' movement had given a decisive impulse to the Bohemian nationalist sentiments that pervaded the Czech nation until contemporary times.

Bibliography (in English)

- "The Hussite Wars", S.Turnbull and A.McBride, Osprey Men-at-Arms nr. 409
- "Jean Ziska", George Sand, Public Domain Book
- "Medieval Handgonnes. The first Black Powder Infantry Weapons", S.McLachlan, Osprey Weapons nr. 3
- "Warrior of God Jan Žižka and the Hussite Revolution", V.Verney, Frontline Books

Cinema

Not to be missed is the Hussite trilogy of 3 colour DVDs in a box set with English subtitles: "Jan Hus", "Jan Žižka" and "Proti všem (Against All)". Filmed between 1954 and 1957, the last two DVDs contain several accurate and powerful battle scenes, particularly of Sudoměř and Vitkov. In some editions the box set is enriched by another DVD on the Battle of Lipany: 'Jan Roháč z Dubé', from 1947. You can find them (with any luck) on eBay or on Amazon.

Miniatures 28mm 1st Corps (formerly Kingmaker), Foundry, Testudo, Essex. 15mm Essex and Museum, painted by Renato Genovese. Photo Renato Genovese.

FIGHTING THE HUSSITES
AS IF IT WAS REAL – A MEMORY

by RENATO GENOVESE

Several years ago, my late friend Valerio "Conan" Laurenzi organized a tournament in Rome. The Early Renaissance period would be played using Arty Conliffe's **Armati** Rulebook. In many tournaments, it is difficult for real historical opponents to clash. However, the period had a certain balance, so the matches took an entirely plausible course. In the second round, my friend Guido Bogi and I were drawn to fight Conan. We had brought an early 15th-century Spanish army, with good cavalry which we partly dismounted, and effective infantry. But the trump card for us were the two "rodeleros" sword and buckler units, classified as LHI, that is, Light-Heavy Infantry, tough in a fray but with good mobility. Arriving at the table, however, we were stunned--because, on the other side of the field, a line of heavily armed wagons looked down on our Spaniards.

Not until then, had a Hussite army appeared on our tournament tables, and we were somewhat puzzled as to how to use our troops. We deployed, and after a quick exchange of artillery fire we began to advance. In addition to the wagons (which Conan affectionately called his "carts") equipped with an artillery piece and several marksmen, the Hussites had two units of cavalry and one of crossbowmen who immediately began to disrupt our advance. Our cannons that were immovable once placed immediately fell silent as our troops were forced to advance into their line of fire to concentrate their assault on the wagenburg. The Hussite pieces, on the other hand, was firing like a beauty. It became clear that our effort, therefore, was to get in contact with the wagons as quickly as possible while hoping not to suffer too many losses from enemy fire. Suddenly, and for the first and only time in my wargamer life, I was struck by the magic of suspension of disbelief and felt as if I had been catapulted onto the battlefield. It was as if everything was real. Ahead of me, as if my vision was fogged with sweat, I glimpsed the wall of wagons erupting fire and hurling deadly crossbow bolts, while other Hussites armed with pole-arms, clubs or war hammers dared us to continue our advance so they could slaughter us.

How our units suffered in the attack! We lost so many to enemy fire before finally, we came into contact. Perhaps in my mind was influenced by the realistic images of the movie Cyrano of Bergerac with Gerard Depardieu in which the Spaniards were trying to dislodge the French with pikes from their field fortifications: a tangle of poles, flags and hand to hand melees at the point of a gun. At this point in the battle, we played our trump card but the swords and shields of our rodeleros were not enough for victory. In fact, they simply became expendable and we sacrificed them, sending them to slaughter but reducing the number of wagons. Our dismounted horsemen finally flanked the wagons on their defenceless side, while our remaining infantry engaged in the frontal melee, and finally the Hussites collapsed.

It took a while to bring myself out of the trance, but I have never forgotten that confrontation, that battlefield and that extrasensory experience. And even now I say, "Thank you great Conan!"

Tips on how I built a Hussite army

by ANTONIO DIMICHELE

At one of the Dadi.com wargame shows in Crema during the 2000 to 2009 period I recall becoming fascinated by a medieval army in 15mm that deployed numerous colourful wagons as if they were each a small fort. At that moment I began to learn the story of the Hussites.

Determined to build a different type of army, I took advantage of Salute and purchased a Hussite army from King Maker marketed by the well-known 1st Corp. However, the army remained in the box until I supplemented it with two additional MDF wagon models from Sarissa precision. The Hussite army of course fielded numerous wagons (wagenburg) and some heavy cavalry as well as light, and heavy infantry units. The wagons were ordinary farm wagons that were "fortified" with parapets that were often embellished with colour and the ever-present Hussite cups.

Being a fan of Impetus, a ruleset that allows you to create excellent diorama-like bases for the wagons I constructed my 28mm miniatures with a base front of 12 cm and depth at least 16 cm. Frankly, the suggested depth seemed excessive to me, but only because the Hussites did not use horse-drawn chariots in combat, but deployed the wagons longitudinally to the enemy. However, after doing some depth testing, I realized that I could deploy the wagon exposing the flank to the enemy and take advantage of the depth for developing dioramas.

A further peculiarity of the Hussites that I discovered was that much of their artillery was deployed in the wagons. The smaller calibres were positioned on the wagons were protected by the pavises, while larger calibre pieces also needed to be deployed behind high cover leading to an innovative solution, howitzers! These first artillery pieces used balls filled with stone or iron, however, it soon became clear that the addition of explosives allowed for greater destructiveness as the projectiles were thrown over obstacles. Until the 15th century there was only talk of "artifizied fochi," that is of projectiles that exploded after being launched. Starting from the time of the Hussite wars, powder-filled hollow balls were used that were detonated by means of a fuse, referred to in French as obus, hence the name howitzer for the related weapon.

For the wagon bases that I placed in a deployment, I tried to give the idea of the circle of wagons which in 28mm is hard and expensive to render for a game. I was helped in this by exploiting two leftover parapets in the Sarissa packs. I have always felt that an empty base with few models is sad so, I filled

them with all the models I had on hand.

Hussite tactics involved anchoring the wheels of the wagons and closing the gaps between them with the placement of paveses, so as to make opposing cavalry charges ineffective. Some wagons, however, were not anchored so as to permit the unexpected movement of heavy cavalry sorties, which of course cannot be ignored by any enemy.

SHOWCASE

Aurelian Leclerc - Carthaginian Elephant
(28mm Relic Miniatures)

Georgios Galazoulas - Bohemond of Taranto
(28mm Caballero Miniatures)

David Imrie - Burgundian Men-at-Arms
(28mm Perry Miniatures)

SOLO MINIATURES RULES

SOLO OR COOPERATIVE WARGAMES RULES FOR MODERN WARFARE

FAST, LETHAL AND CINEMATIC

LEAD YOUR ÉLITE TEAM THROUGH HOSTILE GROUND

AVAILABLE IN PDF AT WARGAMEVAULT.COM

HOSTILE GROUND

Dadi&Piombo

Printed in Great Britain
by Amazon